Apache Essentials
Install, Configure, Maintain

Darren James Harkness

friendsof

DESIGNER TO DESIGNER™

an Apress® company

Apache Essentials:
Install, Configure, Maintain

ISBN (pbk): 1-59059-355-3

Printed and bound in the United States of America 10987654321

Trademarked names may appear in this book. Rather than use a trademark symbol with every occurrence of a trademarked name, we use the names only in an editorial fashion and to the benefit of the trademark owner, with no intention of infringement of the trademark.

Distributed to the book trade in the United States by Springer-Verlag New York, Inc., 175 Fifth Avenue, New York, NY 10010 and outside the United States by Springer-Verlag GmbH & Co. KG, Tiergartenstr. 17, 69112 Heidelberg, Germany.

In the United States: phone 1-800-SPRINGER, e-mail orders@springer-ny.com, or visit http://www.springer-ny.com. Outside the United States: fax +49 6221 345229, e-mail orders@springer.de, or visit http://www.springer.de.

For information on translations, please contact Apress directly at 2560 Ninth Street, Suite 219, Berkeley, CA 94710. Phone 510-549-5930, fax 510-549-5939, e-mail info@apress.com, or visit http://www.apress.com.

The information in this book is distributed on an "as is" basis, without warranty. Although every precaution has been taken in the preparation of this work, neither the author(s) nor Apress shall have any liability to any person or entity with respect to any loss or damage caused or alleged to be caused directly or indirectly by the information contained in this work.

The source code for this book is freely available to readers at http://www.friendsofed.com in the Downloads section.

Credits

Lead Editor: Chris Mills	**Production Manager:** Kari Brooks
Technical Reviewer: Massimo Nardone	**Production Editor:** Ellie Fountain
Editorial Board: Steve Anglin, Dan Appleman, Ewan Buckingham, Gary Cornell, Tony Davis, John Franklin, Jason Gilmore, Chris Mills, Steve Rycroft, Dominic Shakeshaft, Jim Sumser, Karen Watterson, Gavin Wray, John Zukowski	**Compositor:** Dina Quan **Proofreader:** Liz Welch **Indexer:** Michael Brinkman
Project Manager: Tracy Brown Collins	**Artist:** Kinetic Publishing Services, LLC
Copy Edit Manager: Nicole LeClerc	**Cover Designer:** Kurt Krames
Copy Editor: Mark Nigara	**Manufacturing Manager:** Tom Debolski

Cover image courtesy of NASA.

CONTENTS AT A GLANCE

CONTENTS

CONTENTS

ABOUT THE AUTHOR

 **Darren James Harkness** is a creative engineer by day and a gypsy knife-eater by night. He's an old-school web developer who has been hand-developing quality, content-driven sites since 1995. He has an instinctual understanding of web standards and graphic design, along with a solid understanding of back-end development. He has two fat cats, a hyper dog, and a wonderfully supportive partner. You can find Darren online at http://staticred.net/ or in the great white north of Edmonton, Alberta, Canada.

ABOUT THE TECHNICAL REVIEWER

 **Massimo Nardone** holds a master's degree in computer science from the University of Salerno, Italy, and has more than nine years of work experience as a project manager, software engineer, research engineer, chief security architect, and software specialist in project management, mobile, security, and World Wide Web technology for national and international software and telecommunications companies. He also works as visiting lecturer and supervisor for exercises at the Networking Laboratory at Helsinki University of Technology, where he teaches a course on the security of communication protocols. He's an expert on the security standard BS7799 and the PKI and WPKI protocols, for which he holds two international patent applications.

ACKNOWLEDGMENTS

I'd like to thank everyone who made this book possible. And believe me, this book wouldn't have been possible without a few people.

First and foremost is my partner Kirsten, who has been my biggest source of inspiration and strength. Without her support over the past few years, I wouldn't be where I am today. She has also been extremely patient while I put off home renovations to write this book. Thanks baby—you're a goodnik.

Thanks to Kirsten's family, my family, and my good friend Alan, whose server has been my playground for the last few years. Thanks also to all the people who have worked with me and taught me what I didn't know. You know who you are, and there are too many of you to list.

I also want to thank my editors at friends of ED, who made some excellent suggestions while I was writing this book.

Finally, I want to thank all the propellerheads—past and present—who have worked to make Apache and the Web in general the great place that it is. Keep up the good work!

1 INTRODUCTION TO APACHE

Welcome to *Apache Essentials: Install, Configure, Maintain*. A little while ago, I started playing around with Apache, one of the most widely used web servers on the Internet. I had my site hosted on a friend's server in Vancouver, and wanted to know more about the software that was running my domain.

At the same time, I'd just come off a web-design job on which I had relied on two Perl programmers to maintain the company's website, and was completely at their whim any time I needed something fixed or changed. Even a simple restart of the web server was out of my control.

Tired of having to wait on people to do things for me, I decided it was time I started learning about Apache. The problem was that Apache was a completely foreign land to me, complete with sea monsters and wizards. I quickly hit a wall; there was no guide to Apache that talked to me as a designer in terms I could easily understand.

There are plenty of books and websites out there that were full of information about Apache and its configuration; however, they are written with the system administrator or programmer in mind. Designers are smart people, but having to read through pages upon pages of techspeak is enough to scare anyone off.

I'm really quite stubborn, however. I kept struggling through the techspeak, harassed a friend who ran my domain for me, and even installed Apache on my own computer so that I could learn how to use it.

After a little while, I'd learned enough to allow Apache to do what I needed it to do: serve web pages. Sure, I was speaking solely through the use of three-letter acronyms and had an odd desire to stay in dark places—but I think it was worth it in the end. Running a web server under Apache isn't nearly as scary as it appears to be.

Of course, I don't want any of you to go through the same trials I did while learning how to use Apache, and I definitely don't want you to wade through pages of technical jargon. As a result, I'm writing this book for you, the web designer who needs to know more about Apache. I'll strip out all the techspeak, and give you clear instructions on how to get Apache up and running. After that, I'll show you how to set up specific features of Apache, such as virtual domains, scripting languages, and secure websites.

Apache can be run on virtually any commercial operating system—if it has the ability to connect to a network, chances are there's a version of Apache available for it. For this book, however, I'm going to focus only on the most common operating systems: Linux, Windows, and Mac OS X. And, although I'll be explaining differences in these operating systems, I'll be focusing primarily on Linux, since it's most commonly paired with Apache.

Before you dive headlong into the guts of Apache, however, let's do a little review to get you up to speed.

How does a web server work?

It's probably a good idea to start the review by explaining how a web server works. Since this book is intended for the Internet professional, I can assume that you already know a few of the basics—what a web server is, how information is transferred, and so on.

A web server works somewhat like your local librarian at your local reference desk. It works as a front end to a store of information. When a web browser makes a request for a file, the web server will process the request, search for the location of the file requested, then respond with what it found. On the surface, it's pretty simple. Of course, there's a lot of action going on behind the scenes.

The Hypertext Transfer Protocol

A network is best thought of as a combination of communication layers; each layer represents a method of communication, and is assigned a unique TCP port number. There are 65,536 ports in all, and many of those are reserved for known network protocols. One reserved protocol is HTTP, which communicates on port 80. Other examples of TCP ports include POP email (port 110) and FTP (which uses ports 20 and 21).

The HTTP protocol is a common language used for transferring hypertext data between a web server and a web browser. In short, it's how the client and server talk to each other. I'm not going to delve deeply into the protocol, but a sample HTTP transaction would look like this:

```
GET /index.html HTTP/1.1
Host: www.staticred.net
HTTP/1.1 200 OK
Content-Type: text/html; charset=utf-8
Content-Length: length
<DATA>
```

The transaction starts when the browser requests a file from the web server (GET http://www.domain.com/page.htm). When this request is received, the web server checks to see if the file exists at the location specified and if the browser has permission to view the page. If an error is encountered, the web server will return the error to the browser, often followed by a brief explanation of the error. The most common of these errors are 404 (file not found), 403 (forbidden), and 500 (script error).

If everything is fine, the web server will return a 200, then start streaming the content of the file to the browser. Whenever an <img> tag (or any other tag that references additional files, such as the <object> tag) is encountered, the process repeats itself. In the end, the browser receives all of the information contained in the web page, and renders it according to the HTML sent. Given that web pages often reference one or more graphic files, a full HTTP transaction could look like this:

```
GET http://www.domain.com/page.htm
200
<data>
```

```
GET http://www.domain.com/images/header.jpg
200
<data>
```

A full list of the HTTP error codes can be found in the Appendix.

A brief history of Apache

In June 1991, the first web server was born in a room at CERN—a particle physics labora-
tory in Geneva, Switzerland. Then the first version of Hypertext Transfer Protocol Daemon
(httpd) was created. Little did they know they would be opening the door to an entirely
new universe. Or, maybe they did—after all, it was, ironically, a physics lab.

Tim Berners-Lee, the grandfather of the Web, first started working on the basic concept of
linked documents as early as 1980 while on a short contract with CERN. While there, he
created Enquire, a program used privately to store information using random associations.
Though never published, a seed was planted firmly in his mind. When he returned to CERN
in 1989, he brought with him a massive improvement to Enquire.

The World Wide Web (WWW), as Berners-Lee called it, was Enquire on a global scale. The
basic idea behind WWW was to allow a group of high-energy physicists to combine their
individual knowledge into a library of interconnected work. Are you referring to a colleague's paper on quantum mechanics? Instead of merely citing the paper and leaving it
up to the reader to search through a library for it, you could just provide a link to it within
your own paper.

In 1991, after a year or so of internal development at CERN, Berners-Lee released httpd
(the first web server) and WorldWideWeb (the first web editor, and incidentally the first
WYSIWYG editor) to the public at large through the Internet and made his own HTTP
server publicly accessible. The idea hit the 'Net and exploded. According to Berners-Lee,
the load on the CERN web server grew by a factor of ten every year. Berners-Lee spent the
next three years defining the language of the Web—HTML—and further developed
the httpd web server, working heavily with feedback from the Web's early adopters.

Around the same time, the National Center for Supercomputing Applications (NCSA) was
working on its own version of the httpd server. Complaining that the CERN web server was
"too large and complex," Rob McCool worked with several others at NCSA to create a
leaner, simpler version of the web server.[1] He worked on NCSA's web server until 1994,
when—as Apache's timeline states—he "left to get a real job." (In fact, he left to help form
Netscape, and you all know how that turned out.)

---

[1] "Apache History Timeline," The Apache Software Foundation. See www.apache.org/history/
timeline.html.

When Rob McCool left the httpd project, development crept to a halt. By early 1995, as the Internet became more accessible to the general public, use of the Web started booming and webmasters soon discovered that httpd could no longer serve their needs adequately. As a result, in February 1995, eight brave souls started working together to develop the next generation of web servers, Apache. Working from the source code for httpd, these developers started writing patches to the NCSA httpd server (and according to Apache's history, the name was born—"a patchy server"). In April 1995, the group made the first official public release of the Apache web server.[2]

Apache started as an open-source community project. Eight years later, it's a *thriving* open-source community project with hundreds of developers who regularly contribute source material. In 1999, the Apache Software Foundation (ASF) was created as an official entity to help organize developers and provide legal and financial support. Over 27 million domains are powered by Apache, thereby making it the most popular web server on the Internet (compared to just over ten million for Microsoft's Internet Information Server).[3] Apache is available for any operating system that has networking, including Linux, FreeBSD, Windows, Macintosh, OS/2, and even BeOS.

Why should I choose Apache over Internet Information Server?

Apache's long history of stability and security is its largest selling point. As is evident from their website, Apache didn't gain their 27 million served through slick marketing. The Apache Group has earned each and every one of those 27 million web servers through their reputation for releasing exceptionally stable software. Regardless of what platform Apache is released on, it's consistently reliable, stable, and secure.

A proven track record of security

The first thing to consider when putting any kind of server on the Internet is security. I cannot stress this enough. In fact, stop right now, place the book down on your lap, and say this out loud: "I will make sure my web server is secure."

Thankfully, Apache has historically been one of the most secure web servers available. Symantec lists two worms that have affected Apache—and only one of these actually takes advantage of a vulnerability in Apache, and that's in one version of the server for FreeBSD. In contrast, there are literally hundreds of worms that affect IIS on an almost weekly basis. It's become so much of a problem that major media outlets such as CNN have started covering their effects.

---

[2] Ibid.

[3] *"September 2003 Web Server Survey," NetCraft. See* http://news.netcraft.com/archives/2003/09/01/september_2003_web_server_survey.html.

On the rare occasions when major vulnerabilities are found within Apache, a fix is generally made available within days. Since the Apache Group has a very large, very dedicated international team working literally around the clock, they can create, test, and deploy fixes relatively quickly. Sure, Apache can be a little more difficult to configure—but isn't it worth it when you don't have to worry about the next worm taking down your site?

Performance

Performance is an extremely important factor when it comes to your web server. Everybody would like to have the best of the best when it comes to server hardware, but there are some grim realities to face. Not everyone can afford a nice top-of-the-line server; often, existing resources need to be used. Sometimes you may have to make use of existing resources for your web server, especially if your organization's operations aren't explicitly web-based.

Performance is an important selling point when comparing Apache and IIS. Although IIS has slightly higher performance when serving static HTML pages, an Apache-based server surpasses IIS when serving CGI, crunching through a database, or using any other dynamic content. In today's Web, that's an extremely important selling point. In addition, Apache will run on legacy hardware quite happily—just try running IIS on a 486-33.

Flexibility

Apache servers can be extremely flexible—even to the point of offering functionality found in IIS, such as FrontPage extensions and even limited ASP support.

The bottom line: Cost

Possibly the most persuasive argument for Apache is its very attractive total cost of ownership in comparison to IIS. It costs nothing. Apache is distributed free of charge by the Apache Group, whether it's serving personal pages or multiple corporate sites, and each distribution includes its source code. In comparison, Microsoft's arcane licensing scheme for IIS can increase costs swiftly and shrouds its internal workings under a veil of secrecy. The Apache Group believes that keeping the Apache project free is the best way to ensure the quality of its development.

If you combine an installation of Apache with FreeBSD or Linux, you lower your bottom line even further. Sure, there are some learning curves to master with both of these operating systems, but you're rewarded with a more secure, stable, and speedy web server. You might even enjoy the learning process!

What to know before installing Apache

There are a few things you need to consider before installing Apache. These include which operating system to use, what additional software is needed, and which version of Apache to install.

## 1

A useful exercise at this point is to write a quick "needs" document. If you're moving an existing website from a hosted server to your own server, find out how busy your web server has been, and what technologies were being used for it. If you're just starting up, or you don't have access to your web server's statistics, you need to make an estimate on what your server requirements will be.

In both cases, you should ask the following questions:

How popular is the site? How does this translate into hits per month, day, and hour?

The more popular the site, the busier the web server will be. If you're experiencing heavy traffic, the web server will slow down. The best way to mitigate this is by increasing the amount of RAM allocated to the server.

What scripting environments (Perl, PHP, ASP, JSP) are currently being used for the website?

Apache supports most scripting environments, and some will actually run better under Apache. ASP, however, can be a problem area; Apache doesn't directly support it.

How large is the website, and how long do I want to keep server logs for?

Hard drive space is cheap, and a web server is expensive (at least from a storage-space perspective). Add as much hard-drive space as you can afford to. The longer you keep log data, the more information you have to work with when it comes to building website statistics. You'll find more on this in the log file discussion in Chapter 8.

Who do I want to have access to the web server?

This is probably *the* most important question to ask. Anyone who has access to the web server machine also has access to the website stored on it. Though you can secure the directories the website resides in under both Linux and Windows, they aren't 100-percent secure as long as a user has access to the drive.

Which operating system should I use?

There are a number of operating systems that you could potentially select for your Apache installation. Apache offers precompiled binaries (essentially installable applications) for most popular operating systems, such as Windows, Linux, FreeBSD, and even Mac OS X.

Ideally, you should be installing Apache on a true UNIX operating system, such as Solaris. This will offer you the greatest reliability and security (even Microsoft develops a version of IIS for Solaris that runs their Hotmail service). Another excellent (but somewhat costly) option is to install OpenBSD or NetBSD—both of which are well known for their security.

More common, however, is using Linux or Windows for your Apache web server.

Linux is a UNIX-like operating system developed by Linus Torvalds in 1991 in Helsinki, Finland. What started as a graduate-student project has grown into one of the most popular server operating systems on the Internet. Windows, as I'm sure you already know, has become the most prevalent desktop operating system on personal computers.

> *Although you'll go over some of the basic procedures for Windows and Linux, I'd strongly suggest you pick up a reference guide for the operating system you intend to use; it will save you countless headaches.*

For the purposes of this book, I'm going to refer to installing Apache on Linux, and show you the differences with Windows when they come up.

Linux

Linux offers the security and stability of a UNIX system, without the cost; the Linux operating system (as well as the bulk of applications available for it) is placed under the General Public License (GPL) and made available to all, free of charge. It's developed under the philosophy of open source, and as such is generally rock solid and secure.

Since Linux itself consists solely of the basic operating system (and no applications or utilities), it has been packaged with a set of applications and utilities and a method of installation by several organizations. These different packages are called distributions; if you choose to install Linux, the fastest and easiest way is to decide upon a distribution.

There are literally hundreds of distributions to choose from, but only a few are generally accepted by most Linux developers. Accepted distributions include Debian, Red Hat, Slackware, Knoppix, and Gentoo.

Of these, Debian, Slackware, and Red Hat are the oldest and best known. Red Hat has grown to be a large commercial Linux vendor; Red Hat Linux is sold commercially and comes with technical support from Red Hat itself. Slackware and Debian have both remained completely free, but they don't offer the same level of technical support as Red Hat Linux. However, most—if not all—of the information you might need about Linux is readily available on the Web or through newsgroups. Several excellent books are also available—check out the Appendix for more information.

A problem with using Linux, however, is that there will likely be a larger initial learning curve if you aren't already familiar with it. Though Linux can have a graphical interface, through X Windows, most administration is done through a text-only command-line interface. As a result, there's a new set of commands that you'll have to learn and remember.

Pros

- Linux is far more secure than Windows. Due to the open nature of development, vulnerabilities are found and repaired quickly by Linux developers. Patches are often available within hours of a vulnerability being reported.

- With its roots in UNIX, Linux was born and raised a multiuser operating system that was able to handle multiple users and run multiple applications. The Linux developers have had over a decade to hone this ability, and make sure that it handles multiple users with far more ease than Windows.

- The Linux operating system is far more stable and reliable.

- On a non–X Windows system, Linux offers better performance than Microsoft Windows, since very little processing power goes into the display.

- Linux is built for network performance. Every major Linux distribution comes with the network tools needed to get a web server up and running.

- Linux offers far better remote management capability. Several methods, including telnet, Secure Shell (SSH), and remote X Windows, allow you to connect to your server quickly and efficiently.

- Linux is much more modular than other operating systems. The operating system needs only a couple hundred megabytes of disk space, and you only install the applications you want to use on the server.

- Contrary to what Microsoft might like you to believe, support is readily available for Linux. Many distributions will sell you commercial support for a lower yearly cost than a Windows license. Even if you don't pay for support, there are countless tutorials available at sites such as www.ltdp.org, or through newsgroups and email.

- Linux servers rarely have to be rebooted; all system services and applications can be modified or reinstalled without a reboot.

Cons

- Linux offers an unfamiliar interface; most administration is done through the command-line interface.

- Less management support than a Windows installation. Many non-IT managers harbor a suspicion with regards to Linux, since there is no perceived commercial support behind its development. Thankfully, the tide is shifting on this one.

- No single commercial entity is responsible for Linux. However, all major Linux kernel (the core operating system) releases go through a rigorous code-review process before being released. In the past, this was supervised by Linus Torvalds; however, Linux has recently founded the Open Source Development Labs (OSDL), which aims to be the new "gravitational center" for Linux development.

- Graphical administration tools aren't available for all system functions.

- Linux has a larger learning curve than Windows.

- No commercial support is available for some distributions.

Windows

Windows is the second most common choice for installing Apache, since most organizations have a ready supply of Windows servers to use. There are some definite advantages to using Windows; most people are already extremely familiar with the Windows interface, so there's little time required to learn how to administer the server machine.

Pros

- Immediately recognizable user interface for most people.
- Smaller learning curve.
- Graphical tools for administration.
- Many IT professionals have an existing maintenance agreement with Microsoft.

Cons

- Not as secure as Linux; vulnerabilities are routinely found in Microsoft Windows, and these have led to some of the largest virus outbreaks in Internet history.
- Due to the closed development model, it often takes Microsoft days to release a patch after a vulnerability has been reported. Numerous other vulnerabilities may have already been found, but not reported.
- System requirements for a Windows server are often much higher than for a Linux server performing the same tasks.
- Performance doesn't match Linux on the same system specifications; Linux servers offer more reliable network and file operations than Windows, using the same hardware.
- Windows servers are more prone to mysterious crashes and need to be rebooted more often.

The bottom line

My suggestion is to install Apache 1.3 on a UNIX-like operating system, such as Linux or FreeBSD. The examples within this book will draw heavily on this setup (though I'll identify what differences exist for Windows and Apache 2.0 wherever necessary). Installing this combination will give you the highest amount of security, performance, and reliability, and most of these standards exist on the UNIX-like operating system already.

There's a larger learning curve with a Linux system, but it's really worth it in the end. With the plethora of Linux books out there, you should be able to pick it up relatively quickly. I'll list a few in the Appendix for you.

If your organization is strictly Microsoft-only, then I suggest that you install Apache 2.0 on a Windows 2000 system. Apache 2.0 offers better performance than 1.3 on a Windows server, since it has been developed natively. Apache 1.3 is ported from source code that was originally developed for a UNIX-like operating system—and as such it doesn't match Apache 2.0's speed (though it does still match the performance of Microsoft's IIS).

> *Regardless of which operating system and version of Apache you choose, you shouldn't be running any other services on the server. By limiting your server's function to serving web pages, you protect the security of your network (by offering less network-connected applications to exploit) and the performance of your web server (by demanding less attention from your server's processor and memory).*

Where do I get Apache?

It seems like a silly question, but it's important enough to mention here. You should only *ever* get Apache from the official Apache Group website at http://apache.org. Apache is open source; because of this, it's quite easy for a malicious programmer to create a version of Apache with a backdoor program, a Trojan program, or another program with nefarious code embedded inside.

The exception to this rule occurs if you're getting Apache through a trusted Linux distribution, such as Red Hat, Debian, or Slackware.

Should I install from source or binary?

There are two ways to get Apache: source and binary. The source distribution includes the source code for Apache, while the binary distribution includes prebuilt executables for your operating system.

Getting the source code allows you to customize Apache for your particular installation, beyond the included configuration directives. For those users who are extremely security conscious, Apache will allow you to audit the source code for potential problems before they occur. It is, however, a complete nuisance to install from source code on non-UNIX operating systems like Windows.

The binary distribution is the best choice for your purposes; everything is built for you, so you don't have to hunt down a compiler, figure out make files, or do anything else but install the binary to get Apache working. Binaries are available for both Windows and Linux. If you're running Mac OS X, then I have some extremely good news: Apache is already installed for you.

Which version of Apache should I use?

There are currently two versions of the Apache web server available: 1.3 and 2.0. In most software packages, you would immediately go for the higher version number; however, with Apache, that's not always the case.

Stability, security, performance, and reliability are the top considerations when it comes to any kind of server. It's extremely common for systems administrators to keep their web servers one or two versions behind the current version, unless a major security flaw is revealed. Because of this attitude, Apache 1.3 is more commonly installed than 2.0. The 1.3 version doesn't seem to be going away any time soon, however; the Apache Group is still releasing new versions of the 1.3 server.

Apache 2.0 was built to be more scalable than its predecessor. As a result, it was rebuilt from the ground up to take advantage of faster processes, better memory management, and newer technologies. It also integrated many modules that had to be added on to Apache 1.3.

Apache 2.0 also made a large step forward by developing the Windows version natively, instead of porting it from the UNIX source code (as is done with Apache 1.3). This gave the Apache Group a much-needed speed burst under Windows that resulted in better overall performance than Microsoft's own web server, IIS.

For this book, I'm going to focus on Apache 1.3, since it's the most popular version. I'll highlight differences with Apache 2.0 where they exist.

Summing it up

It used to be that your web server was hosted at your local ISP, locked away securely in a little box in the back room. Most companies didn't want to worry about having to look after their own web server; it was better to pay someone to take care of it for them.

But the times, they are a-changin'.

Many companies are bringing their web services on site for reasons that involve both finances and control (among other things, such as security). For most companies with a T1 or higher broadband connection, a web server won't significantly add to the bandwidth load, though a dedicated line is recommended for more popular sites. The benefits from a control point of view are numerous: you gain 24-hour, on-site access to a dedicated web server running your website. This is essential when a rogue CGI takes the website down (but that never happens, right?).

At the same time, the company can't always afford the overhead of a dedicated IT staffer to look after the web server. Nine times out of ten the responsibility of standing up to the task will fall on the company's webhead. And that means you. The next chapter will tell you everything you need to know about installing Apache on both Windows and Linux operating systems. After that, I'll show you how to configure Apache, step by step and feature by feature.

2 INSTALLING APACHE

So you've made the very wise choice to install Apache on your server. But where do you start?

Before you begin

Before you jump right in and install and configure Apache, let's talk about a few things, including system requirements, considerations for Windows and Mac OS X users, and ways to configure your firewall for Apache.

Requirements

Apache has a few system requirements, but they aren't nearly as bad as you might think. The first of these is disk space. Apache needs a jaw-dropping 12 MB to install itself. After it's installed, it needs only 3 MB to run. No, that's not a typo. One of the strengths of Apache is its lean nature. Similarly, you don't need a heck of a lot of RAM or a powerful processor either; Apache will run on as little as 16 MB of RAM on a 486 if you're running a UNIX-based system such as Linux. Of course, that doesn't mean it will run *nicely*. If you follow the system requirements for your operating system, you stand a good chance of being able to run Apache.

I'd suggest giving your Apache web server as much RAM and hard disk space as possible, and spending a little less on the processor unless you plan to place heavy demands on your server or hope to access a database frequently. The more RAM you give Apache, the happier it will be and the faster it will run. Likewise, you never know exactly how much space you'll need on the hard drive for the actual websites running under Apache. If you plan on using a database package such as SQL Server or MySQL, you'll need even more hard drive space.

Windows users

If you're planning on running Apache on a Windows server, you need to know a few things.

First, make sure that your version of Windows is up to date, and that it has the most current service pack installed. This will ensure that all potential security problems are fixed. You can update your copy of Windows through the Windows Update service.

Second, Windows users will want to choose Apache 2.0 over Apache 1.3. I discussed this in Chapter 1. Apache 1.3 was traditionally ported from the UNIX-based source code with little or no optimization for Windows. While it still performed quite well, it wasn't as good as it could have been. This changed with Apache 2.0. Instead of being ported from the UNIX code base, it was rewritten to take advantage of Windows libraries and APIs. As a result, Apache 2.0 is much faster than its predecessor. It's reportedly even faster than Microsoft's own offering, Internet Information Server (IIS).

You may also have to disable the QOS network driver if it's enabled. The QOS network driver monitors the traffic traveling across your network card, and prioritizes it depending on what type of data it is. Unfortunately, it's not as configurable as it could be, and tends to trash Apache traffic on the network.

Set up your firewall

I know this seems like common sense, but you need to configure your firewall to allow people to connect to your Apache server. What? You don't have a firewall? Put down this book **right now** and go get one for your network. You shouldn't be allowing people to access your network without one.

A firewall sits between your network and the Internet and controls all traffic going into and out of your network. Properly configured, a firewall will only allow the traffic that you tell it to into the network. For example, it will block all requests for mail, FTP, or ICQ connections coming from outside the network. By using a firewall, you add a layer of protection to the machines on your network. If nobody can actually reach your machines through the Internet, then they can't be broken into.

You can configure firewalls to allow known services through the network and direct them to machines within the network. If you're configuring a web server on your network, you need to configure your firewall to allow incoming traffic on port 80 (and port 443 if you're going to use SSL) and redirect it to the computer you're installing Apache on. This way, when a request is made to your firewall for a connection to port 80, it actually routes the traffic to and from your Apache web server.

Important note for Mac OS X users

If you're running Mac OS X, and you want to use Apache as your web server, you're in for a bit of a treat. The visionary folks over at Apple have already installed it for you—you simply need to turn on Web Sharing in the System Preferences. It's true. You can completely skip the rest of this chapter, unless you'd like to brush up on the other operating systems, you lucky sot.

Source or binary?

There are two methods of installing Apache on your server: binary or source. The source install contains all of the Apache source code, but isn't ready to use on the server. The binary install is ready to go on your server, but isn't customizable beyond the standard Apache configuration.

The source, Luke

Apache is, and always has been, open-source software. This means that the source code is available for anybody to download, read, modify, and recompile. The source code is a series of instructions and commands that define individual functions (for example, reading the contents of a file and placing it in memory). These functions, when bundled together, create a complete application. However, in order to get to the application from source code, the application has to be compiled (translated from the programming language source code to an executable file and its supporting library files).

One of the strong benefits of using open-source software is security. I talked about this briefly in Chapter 1; Apache's source code is reviewed by literally thousands of eyes, and it's developed by a group of programmers who volunteer their time.

What does that mean to you? It means two things: quality and security. Because Apache is developed in an open environment, the likelihood that bugs, vulnerabilities, and security problems will be found is much, much higher. Even if a bug slips through, it will generally be found and corrected in a matter of days.

But that doesn't tell you why you should choose the source install, does it? The source install is used for one of three purposes:

1. Customizing the application. Some people who are installing the Apache web server may need to make some changes to the source code to meet proprietary needs. For example, they may need to make changes to the way Apache transfers information over the network. Generally, they need to do something that the standard Apache configuration files don't allow them to do. These people have a heck of a lot more programming knowledge than I do.

2. Security auditing. Another reason for downloading the source code is to review it for vulnerabilities and bugs before compiling and running it on your server. Many organizations actually require all software installed on their servers to be audited before being deployed publicly. If this sounds familiar, you may want to download a copy of the Apache source code to hand over to the powers that be.

3. Education. Just like it sounds. If you're trying to learn a programming language, what better way than to use an existing application as an example? Apache has many thousands of lines of code, all publicly open for viewing. It serves as an excellent educational tool for aspiring programmers.

The fact of the matter is that, unless you're running a version of Linux or FreeBSD that doesn't have a package manager (such as Slackware), you won't want to choose the source install. It's mainly there for the propellerheads. You gain some amount of geek credibility by saying you were able to compile an application from source. Of course, you also spend much, much longer getting it to work than if you had just grabbed a binary install in the first place.

The Apache source code can be found at the following URL: www.apache.org/dist/httpd/.

Taking the path less traveled

OK, so you've decided to compile from source. If you really want to travel down this road, follow the process documented by the Apache Group here: http://httpd.apache.org/docs/install.html#traditional.

The benefit of binary

## 2

OK, so getting the source code isn't right for you, so you've decided to do a binary install. This is a precompiled version of Apache for your operating system. There are binary installs available for Windows, Linux, most commercial versions of UNIX, and Mac OS X.

The benefit of the binary file is that you significantly reduce the time between downloading the Apache install and having a running Apache web server. The drawback, of course, is that you completely remove the ability to customize Apache before installing it.

Apache binaries can be found at the following URL: www.apache.org/dist/httpd/binaries/.

A note for Windows users

If you're planning to run Apache on a Windows server, you really don't have a lot of choice between binary and source—unless you have Visual C++ 5.0 or above and a few utilities, including a utility called awk (which is used for matching patterns and manipulating text). Since Visual C++ probably isn't installed on your server, you're better off sticking with the binary install.

Choosing the right package for your operating system

When you get to the download pages for the Apache web server, you're going to encounter some odd names. Apache is available for many operating systems and hardware platforms; as a result, you may often have more than one choice of download for your particular operating system.

Let's take Linux as an example. The following Linux binaries are available for Apache 1.3:

```
apache_1.3.27-ppc-whatever-linux22.tar.gz
apache_1.3.27-s390-whatever-linux22.tar.gz
apache_1.3.27-x86_64-whatever-linux22.tar.gz
```

Respectively, these binaries are for Linux on the PowerPC, the IBM S390, and the Intel x86-based family of processors (the Intel Pentium or Celeron and the AMD Athlon or Duron). Another binary is available for Apache 2.0—the i686-pc. This is a version of Apache that's specifically compiled to take advantages of the features of newer processors, and it will be marginally faster than the nonoptimized binaries.

Choosing the right package is obviously a little easier from a hardware point of view for Windows. However, you'll have to choose between an executable file and an .msi (Microsoft Installer) file. There's little functional difference between the two, so choose the executable file.

How to configure Apache by editing the configuration files

Apache was developed primarily for UNIX-like systems, and then ported to other operating systems. While this is a great thing for stability and security, owing to the robustness of the UNIX-like operating systems, it does have some definite drawbacks. One of these is the fact that it's configured solely through text-based configuration files.

Unlike most Windows or Macintosh applications, there's no Preferences screen where you can set options. Instead, Apache uses a group of configuration files; of these, httpd.conf is the most important, as it contains the bulk of Apache's configuration options.

There's no official method for editing the Apache configuration files. In fact, the Apache documentation never actually tells you how to edit the configuration files. So what high-tech tool do you need to edit Apache's configuration files? A text editor.

That's right—a simple text editor is all you need to configure Apache. On UNIX-based systems like Linux, you can use the ever-useful text editor, vi. vi is available on just about every UNIX-based server out there, and offers a consistent interface between operating systems and platforms. vi is also available for Mac OS X.

The drawback is that it isn't as easy to use as Notepad or other GUI editors. However, you can learn it quite quickly. The following tutorial will help get you going in vi: www.eng.hawaii.edu/Tutor/vi.html.

On a Windows server, you can use either Notepad or Wordpad to edit the Apache configuration files. You can also use any other text editor, such as UltraEdit or even HomeSite. You'll explore Apache's configuration in more detail in Chapter 3. For now, just open the file, take a look around, and get comfortable with your text editor.

Where to find Apache's configuration files

Depending on your operating system, you can find Apache's configuration files in one of the locations listed in the following table:

Operating system	Location of configuration files
Linux	Apache's configuration files are found in the /etc/apache/ directory.
Windows	Apache's configuration files are found in your Apache program folder, in the conf/ subfolder.
Mac OS X	Apache's configuration files are found in the /etc/httpd/ directory.

Where do the files for the website go?

In a sense, it doesn't really matter where you put the files for your website, as long as you tell Apache where they're located in the httpd.conf using the DocumentRoot directive (you'll learn about this in Chapter 3). However, there are a few conventional locations for your main website's files, which are detailed in the following table:

Operating system	Location of web files
Linux	/var/www
Windows	C:\Program Files\Apache Group\Apache\htdocs, C:\Program Files\Apache Group\Apache2\htdocs, or C:\htdocs
Mac OS X	/Library/WebServer/Documents or /Library/WebServer/WebSites/www.domain.com/

Summing it up

By this point, you should have Apache installed and running as a service on your server. You can even test it by opening a web browser on the server and heading to http://localhost/. If everything is happy, you should see a page like this:

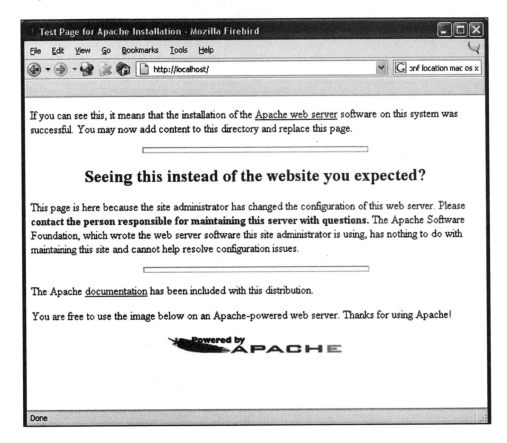

If you do—great! You can move on to Chapter 3, where I'll discuss Apache's basic configuration.

3 BASIC DIRECTIVES

In the previous chapter, I talked about installing Apache and getting it up and running with a basic configuration. Now, let's dive a little deeper into configuring Apache. In this chapter, I'll talk about the following:

- Apache's configuration files
- Server types
- The <Directory> section
- How to configure user directories
- How to change the default index file
- How to rewrite URLs
- How to create custom error messages
- How to authenticate users through Apache
- How to configure access based on an IP address
- How to add new file types
- How to include external configuration files
- How to apply changes to Apache

Apache uses two sets of configuration files. The first set is server-level and is contained mostly in the httpd.conf file. The second set of configuration files is a directory-level configuration file, and supercedes any server-level configuration (if allowed).

> *Before you begin, make sure you back up the original configuration files into a different directory. You'll thank me for this later.*

Server-level configuration

The first set, which you've already been introduced to in the previous chapter, applies to the server as a whole and consists of the following files:

- httpd.conf
- access.conf
- mime.types
- srm.conf

In Linux, this set of configuration files is usually found in /etc/apache. In Windows, this set of files is found in your Apache program folder, in the conf subfolder. There won't be many differences between Windows, Linux, and Mac OS X installations of the Apache web server. However, I'll point them out when they do occur.

Apache reads its configuration files when it first starts. Therefore, any changes to the configuration files will require you to restart the Apache server.

httpd.conf

httpd.conf is the first file Apache looks to for its configuration. As a result, this is where the majority of your configuration options will be found.

The default httpd.conf installed with Apache 1.3 and 2.0 actually contains many more directives than you need; several directives and examples are commented out within the httpd.conf configuration file. This is done by placing a # at the beginning of the line. These commented directives come in very handy. For example, let's say you need to load the mod_userdir module, which allows your users to maintain their own web pages on your server. Instead of trying to figure out what the proper name of the module is, you can just remove the comment character. All of the directives discussed in this chapter will be placed in the httpd.conf, unless specified otherwise.

access.conf and srm.conf

Both access.conf and srm.conf are also left over from older versions of Apache. Most, if not all of the configuration directives that used to be held in these files have now been moved over to access.conf. The srm.conf and access.conf configuration files aren't included in Apache 2.0.

access.conf

The access.conf configuration file is used for the AccessConfig directive. According to the Apache documentation, this file contained the <Directory> sections that now exist in the httpd.conf file. Now, <Directory> sections are included within the httpd.conf.

srm.conf

The srm.conf configuration file is used for the ResourceConfig directive and is used for additional configuration files. This directive is now trumped by the Include directive.

mime.types

The mime.types configuration file is Apache's Rosetta stone. The contents of the mime.types file matches file extensions to content types. For example, HTML files have the following entry in the mime.types configuration file:

```
text/html            htm html xhtml
```

If you need to add a new file type, this is the place to do it. I'll talk about it a little more in the "Adding New File Types" section of this chapter.

Directory-level configuration

If the AllowOverride directive is not set to None, you can specify certain configuration options at the directory level, through the .htaccess file. .htaccess is most often used for authenticating users in a protected directory, or changing the default index files within a directory.

The directives contained within the .htaccess file take precedence over directives in the httpd.conf configuration file, and apply to all subdirectories contained within.

A typical .htaccess file looks like this:

```
DirectoryIndex index.html index.htm
AuthName "StaticRed Statistics...."
AuthType Basic
AuthUserFile /home/staticred/public_html/stats/.htpasswd
require valid-user
```

Server types

The ServerType directive is included in Apache 1.3 for backwards compatibility with older UNIX-based versions of Apache. By default, Apache is set to a stand-alone server, which means Apache will run as a separate application on the server. However, you can also configure Apache to run as a daemon, which is similar to a Windows service. Running Apache in stand-alone mode is recommended for performance reasons.

> *The ServerType directive isn't available in Apache 2.0.*

Configuring a domain

You should make sure that your Apache configuration deals with setting options for your main domain in the httpd.conf configuration file. Though I covered this briefly in Chapter 2, I'll go into it in greater detail in the following sections.

Basic configuration

The first thing you need to do is define what Apache's root directory for web files is. This is done through the ServerRoot directive. Although you can configure Apache for multiple domains, there will always be a primary domain that the server defaults to. In most installations of Apache, the default web directory is /var/www under Linux, but it's located in the htdocs folder within your Apache program directory under Windows. On a Linux system, you would set the following for the ServerRoot directive:

```
ServerRoot /var/www
```

Under Windows, you usually have to enclose the path to your web documents within quotations. It would look something like this:

```
ServerRoot "C:/Program Files/Apache/htdocs"
```

If the root directory is within the Apache program folder, you can specify a relative path. In this case, the ServerRoot directive would look something like this:

```
ServerRoot htdocs
```

After you've configured the main document root directory for Apache, you need to specify options for it by creating a <Directory> entry. This sets the actual configuration of your website within Apache, and controls what access files on your website have.

```
<Directory /var/www/>
    Options Indexes Includes FollowSymLinks MultiViews
    AllowOverride All
    Order allow,deny
    Allow from all
</Directory>
```

This can be broken down pretty easily: In the <Directory> directive, you need to specify the directory you're configuring. Since you want to configure the main domain, you should match the DocumentRoot directory, /var/www. If you want to specify options for a different directory, say /cgi-bin, you would add another section, like this:

```
<Directory /var/www/cgi-bin>
    Options Indexes Includes FollowSymLinks ExecCGI MultiViews
    AllowOverride All
</Directory>
```

This section would allow CGI files to be executed in the /cgi-bin directory, but not within the rest of your website. This allows you to contain all script files to a single directory, thereby making it easier to audit what scripts are being run on your Apache server.

When you configure a directory, you also configure all subdirectories contained within it. So, when you make changes to /var/www, the changes would be applied to /var/www/images as well. In order to give special configurations to individual subdirectories within your main DocumentRoot, you'll have to create separate <Directory> entries for each one.

Directory options

After you've told Apache which directory you want to set options for, you need to tell it which options to configure the directory with. There are many options that you can set on a directory.

Option	Description	Should I use it?
All	Enables all options with the exception of MultiViews. This is the default setting.	If you're looking for a quick way to configure a directory, and you're not concerned about performance or security, then yes. Otherwise, specify your options manually.
ExecCGI	Allows CGI files to be executed in the directory. This should only be enabled for directories containing scripts, because enabling it for all directories will cause Apache to take a hit on its performance.	You should use this only for directories that contain CGI files. Note that you do not need to use this setting for PHP files within a directory.
FollowSymLinks	If this is enabled, the server will follow symbolic links within a directory. Symbolic links are similar to Windows shortcuts; they're pointers to other files or directories within a UNIX system. This option is ignored if used within a <Location> directive.	Yes. This allows you to set up shortcuts to files and directories, without having to duplicate documents on your system. A side benefit of this is that you only need to edit the original file, and all symbolic links will automatically be updated.
Includes	If Server Side Includes (SSI) are enabled on your Apache server, this option will allow HTML files to use all functions of SSI, including the #exec function.	No—for security reasons, I would suggest using the IncludesNOEXEC option. This option allows you to use SSI to include header and footer files within your HTML documents.
IncludesNOEXEC	This option is identical to the Includes option, but doesn't enable the #exec function. The #exec function allows an HTML document to execute a system command.	Yes. This option is identical to the Includes option, but removes the #exec function from SSI.

(Continued)

Option	Description	Should I use it?
Indexes	If no documents matching the ones specified in the DocumentIndex directive are found (index.html, for example), Apache will return a formatted directory listing of the requested URL.	This option can be enabled or disabled, depending on the level of security that you want on your Apache server. If this option is enabled, it will show users a listing of the files within a directory. Though this is fine for most applications, you may not want it for others (for example, a directory that contains script files). If this option isn't enabled, a request for a directory that doesn't contain a DocumentIndex file will return a 403 forbidden error.
MultiViews	The MultiViews directive searches for files matching the requested file. For example, if a requested file doesn't exist on the server, Apache will display the closest match.	This is definitely recommended so that you can catch any mild typos made by people requesting URLs.
SymLinksIfOwnerMatch	This is identical to the FollowSymLinks option, but only follows the symbolic link if it's owned by the same user on the system as the original directory. If the symlink is not owned by the same user, the symbolic link will not be followed.	It's a good idea to enable this option if you want to preserve security within your system. For example, if you allow users on your system to have their own websites through user directories, it's a good idea to enable this option.

Configuring user directories

In some instances, you may want to allow users on the web server to host their own web content without opening up the main website to them. For example, on an intranet, you may want to allow users to maintain content for their associated departments or working groups.

A typical user directory URL looks like this:

```
http://www.domain.com/~username/
```

It's important to note the tilde character (~) in the directory name. This is what tells Apache that this is a user directory, and what directs it to the right location on the server. The actual web content for each user directory is stored within a public_html folder within the user's home directory. On UNIX-based systems, this is often /home/username/ or /var/home/username/.

User directories are configured in three steps. First, you have to load the mod_userdir module; second, you have to configure the mod_userdir module to specify the location of the users' HTML directory; third, you need to configure the user directories' options.

> *Never—wait, I need to make this more emphatic—***NEVER*** set the user's HTML directory to be their main user directory. If you do, all files within the directory will be readable by anyone who can load the website. Instead, create a public HTML directory (such as public_html) within the user directory.*

Loading the mod_userdir module

The mod_userdir module is included with the basic installation of Apache 1.3 and Apache 2.0 and is enabled by default.

The following line should be added to your httpd.conf configuration file:

```
LoadModule mod_userdir.c
```

Configuring the mod_userdir module

Next, you need to tell Apache where the user directories are. The following is an example:

```
<IfModule mod_userdir.c>
    UserDir public_html
</IfModule>
```

Configuring the user directories

You then need to configure the <Directory> section for the user directories. Like the main <Directory> section earlier, this contains all the configuration options for the user's home directories. A good idea here is to limit what the users can do by default, including executing script files. If a user needs to use something that isn't allowed by default, you can audit their request and create a special section for their directory if you feel they should be allowed the special configuration.

One thing you'll notice here is that a wild card (the asterisk) is used when defining the directory. The wild card will match all directories in the given format. For example, /home/fred/public_html will be treated exactly the same as /home/wilma/public_html. The following <Directory> section will allow SSI, symbolic links (if the owners match), and will generate a directory listing if there are no DocumentIndex files in the user's directory. It also puts some minimal security in place with regards to HTTP requests—only GET, POST, OPTIONS, and PROPFIND are allowed—HTTP requests that might possibly alter content are denied.

```
<Directory /home/*/public_html>
    AllowOverride FileInfo AuthConfig Limit
    Options MultiViews Indexes SymLinksIfOwnerMatch IncludesNoExec
    <Limit GET POST OPTIONS PROPFIND>
        Order allow,deny
        Allow from all
    </Limit>
    <Limit PUT DELETE PATCH PROPPATCH MKCOL COPY MOVE LOCK UNLOCK>
        Order deny,allow
        Deny from all
    </Limit>
</Directory>
```

> *Under Windows, the user directory isn't automatically discovered. As a result, you have to specify the full path to the user directory. By default, this is set to C:\Program Files\Apache Group\Apache\users\.*

Changing the default index file

By default, Apache looks for the index.html file when it's loading a directory request. In order to change its default behavior, you must use the DirectoryIndex directive. For example, if you wanted the server to load welcome.htm instead of index.html when a directory request is received, you would use the following:

```
DirectoryIndex welcome.htm
```

DirectoryIndex is most often used in the context of .htaccess, but can also be specified within a <Directory> section in the httpd.conf configuration file.

Rewriting URLs

Often in a redesign situation, you'll need to move the contents of one directory to another. On a mechanical basis, this is pretty easy and doesn't pose a problem—you just copy the files from one location to another. The only thing you really need to change is your own HTML, so that users can find the new location.

One tried and true method used by webmasters from time immemorial is to replace the old HTML file with one that tells the user that the file has been moved to a new location, followed by a request to update their bookmarks to match the new location.

But this causes a couple of problems. First, the user is inconvenienced, since they have to go an extra step to find the content they were looking for—and some may not understand immediately that the content has been moved—they'll just see it isn't there. The second problem is much more serious, however. Search engines won't follow your links. They'll simply see that the content has changed, and that it no longer matches the search terms the page used to be associated with.

Apache supplies an alternative in the mod_rewrite module. This module comes with Apache 1.3 and 2.0, and allows you to create custom rules to rewrite document requests. The mod_rewrite module works by capturing a request and comparing it against the Apache configuration file. If a match is found, it will process the rule and redirect the user to the supplied location.

To load the mod_rewrite module, place the following in your httpd.conf configuration file:

```
LoadModule rewrite_module /usr/lib/apache/1.3/mod_rewrite.so
```

One of the most common uses of the rewrite rule is to fix the "trailing slash problem." The trailing slash problem can be summarized like this: By default, Apache treats all incoming requests as file requests, unless they have a trailing slash. For example, if a user requests http://www.domain.com/fred, Apache would look for a file called fred. If a file called fred doesn't exist, but a directory named fred does, Apache will report a 404 file not found error to the user. If the user requests http://www.domain.com/fred/, Apache will find the fred directory, then load the configured DocumentIndex file for it.

```
RewriteEngine On|Off
RewriteBase <directory>
RewriteRule <source> <destination>
```

> For more information about regular expressions, visit Stephen Ramsay's "Using Regular Expressions" at http://etext.lib.virginia.edu/helpsheets/regex.html.

Rewriting URLs at the server level

If you're making permanent global changes to the location of a document or directory, you should place the rewrite rules within your domain's main <Directory> section.

```
RewriteRule <pattern> <destination> [flag]
```

RewriteRule uses registry expressions to match file and directory names. Registry expressions allow you to match specific terms, such as "index.html" or more vague terms such as "all files that have 'index' in their names". A registry expression tutorial can be found at http://gnosis.cx/publish/programming/regular_expressions.html.

Example

Let's say that you had to move the location of a product's support page from within the product's directory to a new location that pulls information out of a database.

Originally, the page was located at www.domain.com/widget5/support/index.html. Now, if you want users to go to www.domain.com/support/product.php?pid=widget5, you would add the following to the <Directory /var/www> section:

```
RewriteEngine On
RewriteBase /widget5/support/
RewriteRule ^index\.html    /support/product.php?pid=widget5
```

Rewriting URLs at the directory level

There are occasions for which you may not want to place a rewrite rule within the main server configuration file. In these instances, you'll want to place the rewrite rules within the .htaccess file.

An alternative to mod_rewrite

An alternative to using the mod_rewrite module is to use Redirect the mod_alias module. This module isn't quite as powerful as the mod_rewrite module, but definitely does the trick for temporary redirections.

The mod_alias module works similarly to the mod_rewrite module, but uses different directives and a slightly different format. There are four major directives used when employing the mod_alias module: Redirect, RedirectMatch, RedirectTemp, and RedirectPermanent.

Redirect

The Redirect directive takes a specific match and redirects it. For example, if you had moved the /product folder to /products, you would write the following rule in your .htaccess file:

```
Redirect /product/ http://www.domain.com/products/
```

The Redirect directive can take one of four additional options, which are laid out in the following table.

This option	Tells the client
Permanent	The resource has been permanently moved to the destination address. This is equivalent to HTTP error code 301.
Temp	The resource has been temporarily relocated to a new destination. This is the default behavior of the Redirect directive. This is equivalent to HTTP error code 302.
Seeother	The resource has been replaced with new content at the destination address. This is equivalent to HTTP error code 303.
Gone	The requested page has been permanently removed. This is equivalent to HTTP error code 401. If this option is selected, no destination is required.

RedirectMatch

This is functionally identical to the Redirect directive, but allows you to use regular expressions when defining your source. For example, you can match all GIF files on your server and redirect them to JPG files by using the following expression:

```
RedirectMatch (.*).\.gif$ http://www.domain.com/$1.jpg
```

RedirectTemp

The RedirectTemp directive is identical to the Redirect directive.

RedirectPermanent

The RedirectPermanent directive is identical to the Redirect directive.

Redirecting URLs to an external web server

The mod_rewrite module also allows you to redirect URL requests to an external web server. This is useful if you're moving content from one domain to another, for example, between two intranet servers.

Creating custom error messages

By default Apache opens a very plain page when an error is encountered. As you can see in the following figure, the default Apache error message gives little detail about the error.

As you can see, the error message isn't very descriptive or helpful for the end user; there's no explanation of why the user got the error, and no way for the user to find what he or she was looking for. It's also a showstopper for search engines, whose spiders will be stopped dead in their tracks by the 404 message, and will not continue to catalog your site.

Example: useit.com

Jakob Neilsen's useit.com hs a very useful 404 page, pictured below.

Jakob explains how the user may have arrived at this page by explaining the common mistakes made on the site. He then goes on to display the most popular pages on the website along with a link to the home page, so that users can move quickly to the content they were expecting. Finally, he provides search functionality on the page, so that users can search for content that isn't covered by the home page or most popular links.

ErrorDocument syntax

Error documents are handled in the following format:

```
ErrorDocument <error number> <file to display>
```

To load the file /errors/404.php when a 404 error is encountered by the server, you would place the following within your httpd.conf:

```
ErrorDocument 404 /errors/404.php
```

You can create error documents for virtually every HTTP error code, but the most common are detailed in the following table.

Error code	Description
404	File not found. The user has requested a URL that doesn't exist on the server.
403	Forbidden. The user has requested a URL that he doesn't have access to.
500	Internal server error. This is one of Apache's more vague errors, because it's used to cover a wide range of problems. However, bad scripts on the server most often cause a 500 error. Check your error.log and access.log files and try to track down the problem.
401	Authorization required. The user has attempted to log in to a directory secured by Apache's authentication and didn't have the proper username and/or password.

Redirecting to external error documents

You can also redirect users to external error documents in the ErrorDocument directive. This is most useful for the 401 and 403 errors, for which users aren't allowed access to the requested URL.

For example, if you're running an employee extranet at http://employees.domain.com, and you're employing Apache's authentication module, you can have failed logins redirected to http://www.domain.com/errors/401.php. The syntax would look like this:

```
ErrorDocument 401 http://www.domain.com/errors/401.php
```

Authenticating users through Apache

Apache offers basic authentication for users on your website, which lets you password-protect directories on your web server. This can be a very useful feature for employee- or member-only sections of your website, and is used by a large majority of web developers.

A note on basic authentication: It's just that—basic. There's no encryption offered through basic authentication, which means that the username and password, as well as the information contained within the protected directory, travel as plain text through the Internet. Though this lack of encryption doesn't pose a problem most of the time, it does create the potential for a "man-in-the-middle" attack on your data.

One way to avoid sending username and password data in clear text is to configure digest authentication, which uses a basic encryption method to protect the password. This method will not protect the actual data in the protected directory from being intercepted, however. If you want a truly secure authentication method, you should employ SSL and a proprietary login method using a scripted language and local database connection.

The following table details the Apache directives that relate to authentication.

Directive	Values	Recommended setting
AuthName	Any string value, in quotation marks.	Enter something descriptive of the directory being protected.
AuthType	Basic—username and password are used to authenticate the user. Digest—same as basic authentication, but the password is encrypted.	Use Basic, because this is the authentication most supported by all major browsers. Digest authentication is buggy in Internet Explorer.
AuthGroupFile	Specifies the location of the group file.	Do not include this directive unless you're configuring access for a large number of users.
AuthUserFile	Specifies the location of the password file for use with Basic authentication.	The password file is commonly named .htpasswd. I'd recommend sticking with convention on this one. Good security practice recommends that you store your .htpassword file outside of your web-accessible directories in order to avoid a direct request.
AuthDigestFile	Specifies the location of the password file for use with Digest authentication.	Using this directive isn't recommended at this time. Not all browsers support Digest authentication.
User	Specifies that a distinct user or users are allowed to access the protected area.	Unless you're keeping a central .htpasswd file, and want to further limit access to a protected directory, you don't need this directive.
Require	valid-user, user *username,* group *groupname,* file-owner, file-group	The most commonly used option is required-user, since most people choose to maintain separate .htpasswd files.

(Continued)

Directive	Values	Recommended setting
Satisfy	Any, All	By default, Apache chooses the All option. However, if you want users to meet one requirement or another, use the Any option.

Basic configuration

Configuring basic authentication is a two-part process. First, you must set up your password file. This file is most often named .htpasswd, and should reside in a non-web-accessible area on your web server so that the file isn't accessible to web users. Second, you need to configure an .htaccess file in the directory you wish to protect.

A standard setup for basic authentication looks like this:

```
AuthName "Protected Statistics Directory.  Employees only."
AuthType Basic
AuthUserFile /var/www/stats/.htpasswd
Require valid-user
```

Configuring access based on IP address

In some instances, restricting access based on a username and password isn't enough. It won't act as enough of a deterrent for the tenacious hacker. You may need to restrict access based on where the user is coming from. For example, you may need to restrict access to an intranet directory for users from your network, or you may want to restrict access to a customer directory to a specific client's site.

The Order, Deny, and Allow directives control access based on a user's IP address. These directives can be placed within a <Directory> section in the httpd.conf configuration file, or within an .htaccess file within a specific directory on your web server. The order in which you write the Order, Deny, and Allow directives is very important; Apache checks the IP address where the URL request originated from in the order specified by the Order directive. Thus the following

```
Order deny, allow
Allow from 192.168.0
Deny from all
```

will deny all users, regardless of where they come from, whereas

```
Order allow, deny
Allow from 192.168.0
Deny from all
```

will allow users from within the 192.168.0.x network, and deny access to all others. In order to test it, try to connect to the website from outside your network. You can do this from the comfort of your own workstation by attempting to view the page through an anonymous web proxy such as `http://anonymizer.net`, or by simply attempting to run the site through the W3C's validation service.

Example: Restricting access to an intranet directory

Let's take the example of restricting access to the /intranet/ directory on your website to users within your domain. Chances are that your internal network uses an IP addressing scheme of 192.168.0.x. The following would be placed in an .htaccess file within the /intranet directory on your website:

```
Order allow, deny
Deny from 192.168.0
Allow from all
```

Adding new file types

Apache generally knows only a few file extensions as web content: .html, .htm, .shtml, and .cgi in general. If it encounters a file extension it doesn't know, Apache treats the file as a plain text document, and displays it as such. While this is good most of the time, there are occasions on which you'll actually want to use a different file extension. For example, you have to tell Apache how to handle files with the .php file extension when adding PHP files to your website. Likewise, you have to tell it how to handle files with a .cfm extension if you add ColdFusion to the site.

The installation program for packages such as PHP and ColdFusion often handle this, but you should have an idea of how to set up new file types in Apache just in case something goes wrong. It's also useful for creating custom file extensions if you want to obscure the programming language being used by scripts, for example.

Configuring mime.types

The first step in creating new file types is to add a new entry to the mime.types configuration file or add to an existing entry. For example, if you wanted files with a .content extension to be treated as HTML files, you would need to find the text/html file, and add the following:

```
text/html               htm html xhtml content
```

Including external configuration files

The Include directive in Apache allows you to maintain several Apache configuration files separately, which are then included as part of the main httpd.conf. This is an extremely useful directive, especially in situations in which you're running multiple domains on a single host, or if you want users to have the ability to access and change the configurations for their directories on the server.

Creating multiple configuration files lets you keep the core configuration of the web server safe from prying fingers, while letting people change configurations for their own services. It's also an extremely effective way of managing your server's configuration. For example, you could set up several different configuration profiles by creating multiple configuration files, which let you adjust Apache's settings depending on the expected load. Alternatively, you could create a "safe" configuration for troubleshooting purposes.

Applying changes

Once you've made changes to your Apache configuration files, you need to apply them. If you've edited an .htaccess file, then there's no further steps for the configuration changes to take—they will be loaded the next time the directory is requested.

However, if you've made changes to the httpd.conf file or files included in the httpd.conf configuration file, you'll have to restart Apache in order for the changes to take. Thankfully, the Apache Group has included tools so you can do just that. In Linux, Apache is controlled by an utility called apachectl. To restart the Apache server using the apachectl utility, run the following:

```
apachectl graceful
```

There is a restart command; however, if you use graceful to restart your web server, you'll avoid disconnecting users who are currently on the server. Two other commands are available: shutdown and start. You should only use these commands if you expect to take the web server down for an extended period of time for maintenance, and if you do not want **any** connections made to it.

Windows users have a graphical utility included with the Apache installation that will allow them to stop and start the user with a single mouse click. This utility sits in the system tray when Apache is running. To load the maintenance screen, double-click the icon. The Apache Service Monitor, shown in the following figure, will appear.

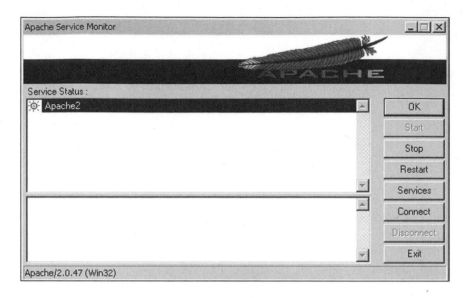

To restart the server, simply select your Apache server and click the Restart button.

Summing it up

You now have Apache installed and configured to its defaults. You're almost ready to go live with your website! In the next chapters, you'll use the directives you've learned in this chapter to set up virtual hosts, you'll learn about modules, log files, and scripting languages, and you'll set up a secure server.

4 VIRTUAL HOSTS

Ah, the wonders of modern technology.

In the early days of the Web, it wasn't very common for people to have their own domain names. Hosting was hard to come by, and when you could find it, it was anywhere from $50 to $300 a month, plus up to $75 a year for the domain name itself. I recall that one ISP in my hometown was selling a luxury hosting package that included 300 KB of storage and 150 MB of traffic for $100 a month—a far cry from the discount hosting of today!

As a result, most websites had impossibly long directory structures to remember in order to access them directly, but you only needed one server machine to run the web server on. For example, the first website I really published anything on was a literature journal located at `http://mypage.direct.ca/b/bbell/djh/solas/`—not exactly the most memorable domain.

Obviously, this has changed in the last few years and the amount of registered domain names have increased dramatically to the point where it's hard to find a domain name that *isn't* already registered. The literary journal I mentioned earlier evolved into something that now sits at `http://nasty.cx`, which I think you'll agree is a far more memorable domain name. I own two other domain names as well: `www.staticred.net` and `www.staticred.com`.

As a result of the explosion in domain-name ownership, the Apache Group needed to add a virtual hosting feature that granted multiple domains the ability to share a server, instead of placing each domain on its own individual server. As far as both the domain and the browser are concerned, the domain has its own dedicated server, and the need for long convoluted paths has been removed. Apache's virtual-hosting feature has become one of its most important. It's used by countless web-hosting providers as a cost-savings measure.

Virtual hosting works by listening to the requests sent to the Apache web server, which determines which domain is being accessed, and then directing the traffic to the proper directory in order to find the requested files. In this way, you can completely segregate websites on your server, without worrying about things such as file conflicts.

In this chapter, I'll talk about what you need to do to configure virtual hosts. I'll start with a discussion of what virtual hosts are, and what you have to do on your server to configure them.

DNS configuration

A DNS server works by translating a readable hostname to the numerical IP address the hostname actually resides at. IP addresses are fundamental to how the Internet works, but they aren't very memorable, because people generally remember natural language names with much more ease than a string of numbers. Adding hostnames allowed people to assign natural language names to a server, thereby making it much easier to remember which server is where. For example, my own domain, staticred.net, actually resides on a computer with an IP address of 209.174.19.10.

You need to set up your DNS for the domains that your web server is going to host. If the DNS server doesn't know that a domain is located within its file system, there's no way it will know to pass that information on to Apache—it will simply say, "Nope, that domain isn't here!" and reject the traffic. The DNS server doesn't necessarily have to live on the same machine as Apache, but it does have to know which machine Apache is on.

Configuring the DNS only becomes a major issue if you're setting up multiple domain names—for example, staticred.net and staticred.com. For subdomains—nasty.staticred.net, for example—you can skip to the Apache configuration section, since you don't need to do any special DNS trickery to make them work. You can also skip to the next section if your Internet access provider manages your DNS; they will add the new domain names to their own DNS server at your request.

Shelves of books have been written on DNS configuration, so I won't go into great detail about how it all works. Suffice it to say that setting up your DNS is really quite important in order for your virtual hosts to *actually* work. If your DNS is hosted off-site, or you have some in-house geeks that can handle this for you, you can skip this section.

For this section, I'm going to focus on the most popular DNS package that's available for Linux, Windows, and virtually every other major operating system out there. BIND has been running the Internet for over 20 years, and is currently up to version 9.

To configure BIND (Linux, Windows, and Mac OS X)

Like Apache (and pretty much every server product for Linux), BIND is available free of charge from the Internet Software Consortium (ISC). BIND is available for most common operating systems, including Linux and Windows, and is the most commonly used software package for DNS. It's likely that you already have an installation of BIND on your server, or that your access provider has an installation of BIND configured for you.

If you can, get someone else to set this up for you. Seriously. You're getting yourself into some pretty major propellerhead territory if you try and do this yourself, and there's a lot of opportunity to mess things up here. I'm not even going to pretend that this one is easy. On the bright side, you earn yourself some major geek points if you can pull this one off.

If you still insist on doing it yourself, or you have no one else to do it, I highly suggest you check out the Linux Network Administrator's Guide, which is available online at www.faqs.org/docs/linux_network/x-087-2-resolv.named.html. You should also check the unofficial FAQ maintained by the comp.protocols.tcp-ip.domains newsgroup, which is available online at www.intac.com/~cdp/cptd-faq/. BIND, if it isn't already installed on your server, can be found at ftp://ftp.isc.org/isc/MIRRORS/.

Sample BIND configuration

Virtual domains are configured in two parts. The first part is configured in your named.conf file, which can generally be found in the /etc/bind/ directory on Linux and the C:\WINNT\System32\dns\etc directory under Windows 2000. A sample entry would look like this:

```
zone "staticred.net" {
    type master;
    file "pri/staticred.net";
};
```

This entry essentially tells BIND that there's a domain that it should be listening for, and that its options are stored in a zone configuration file at pri/staticred.net. This file lives in the /var/cache/bind directory, and contains the second part of your domain configuration.

The contents of the zone configuration file are a little trickier. Here's a sample:

```
; BIND data file for staticred.net zone
$TTL 604800
@   IN  SOA ufies.org. staticred.staticred.net. (
            1999051046      ; Serial
                  7200      ; Refresh
                  1800      ; Retry
                604800      ; Expire
                 21600 )    ; Default TTL
; Nameserver records
    IN  NS  ns1.ufies.org.
    IN NS   ns6.gandi.net.
; Host addresses
staticred.net.      IN  A   65.110.12.164
www                 IN  CNAME staticred.net.
staticred.net.      IN  MX  0 mail.staticred.net.
staticred.net.      IN  MX  10 staticred.com.
; Aliases
nasty               IN CNAME www
```

You can follow this template to configure your own domain, but you need to pay attention to the following options:

Option	Description
@ IN SOA *nameserver domain* (	This opens the zone configuration file for the domain and sets the basic networking options for it.
Serial *serial*	The domain name's serial number within BIND. This can be any unique number, but the rule of thumb used by most administrators is to use today's date, with two digits following it. For example, if you were creating a new domain on December 10, 2003, the serial number would be 2003121000. This number must be incremented any time you make a change to the zone configuration file. In the previous example, you would change the serial number to 2003121001 if you made a change.
IN NS *nameserver*	This configures the domain's primary and secondary DNS servers. The primary DNS is listed first, and is followed by the secondary DNS.
hostname IN A *IP address*	This configures the DNS resolution, and tells BIND what IP address the domain should be attached to.
subdomain IN CNAME *domain*	This sets up subdomains for the domain, and points traffic to the main domain if it's requested. It's highly recommended that you set up the www subdomain this way.
domain IN MX *domain*	This configures mail relays for the domain. If you need to configure this, refer to the Linux Network Administrator's Guide.

4

To configure DNS on Windows 2000/XP

Sadly, configuring DNS under Windows 2000 or Windows XP isn't any easier. Microsoft also offers DNS configuration for its server-level operating systems, which make use of the Microsoft DNS Server. The Microsoft DNS Server is only available for Windows 2000 Server, Windows NT 4, and Windows XP Professional. More information can be found here: http://support.microsoft.com/default.aspx?scid=http://support.microsoft.com:80/support/kb/articles/q172/9/53.asp&NoWebContent=1.

An alternative to the Microsoft DNS Server is DeEnesse, a more user-friendly DNS server based on BIND. A free trial can be found here: http://cyberspacehq.com/products/Deenesse/home.shtm.

I would personally suggest downloading the Windows NT/2000 version of BIND and configuring that. A good article on configuring BIND 8 for Windows can be found here: www.calwell.ca/articles/a0012.php.

There are also many tools out there to help you manage your DNS server. A good list can be found at www.dns.net/dnsrd/tools.html. Two very good tools are DeEnesse, a DNS configuration tool for Windows, and Webmin, a web-based configuration tool for Linux and Mac OS X.

Apache configuration

Configuring Apache for multiple domains is much simpler than configuring BIND. In fact, if you've already read through the basic directives chapter, you already know most of it. Each virtual host has the same configuration options as a single hosted domain, as far as Apache is concerned. The only difference is the domain name the configuration points to and the directive used to denote the domain's configuration.

Name-based vs. IP-based virtual hosting

There are two types of virtual hosting: name-based and IP-based. IP-based virtual hosting requires every virtual host to have its own unique IP address on the server, whereas name-based virtual hosts can share a single IP address. As a result, name-based virtual hosting is far more common than IP-based virtual hosting.

However, there are some drawbacks to using name-based virtual hosting. According to the Apache documentation, name-based virtual hosting works because the client passes along the domain name as part of its HTTP request. Under HTTP 1.1 this is required; however, under older versions of the HTTP protocol, this is not required. Older browsers that don't add the hostname into their HTTP requests will result in the domain not being found by Apache.

If you plan on using SSL with a virtual host, you *must* use IP-based virtual hosting in order for the SSL connection to be made. I'll discuss this more in Chapter 7.

Configuring Apache

You can configure virtual hosts directly within the httpd.conf file, or you can create separate files for each virtual host, then import them into the httpd.conf via that Import directive. If you want to maintain central control over your Apache configuration, then place the virtual host configurations within your httpd.conf. However, if you want users on your system to have the ability to change their own Apache configurations, or you want to make domain maintenance more efficient, you should create separate files for each domain. For example, you would create staticred.com.conf for the staticred.com domain, whereas you would create staticred.net.conf for the staticred.net domain.

The *only* difference between a configuration for a virtual host and one for a regular domain is the <VirtualHost> directive and its supporting directives, <ServerName> and <ServerAlias>. The actual configuration of a virtual host is identical to setting up your main domain.

4

Sample Apache configuration

Here's a sample configuration for a virtual host in Apache. My domain, staticred.net, is virtually hosted by a colleague of mine, along with several other domains.

```
NameVirtualHost 192.168.1.34
<VirtualHost 192.168.1.34>
    ServerAdmin webmaster@staticred.net
    DocumentRoot /home/staticred/public_html
    ServerPath /home/staticred/public_html
    ServerName staticred.net
    ServerAlias www.staticred.net
    ErrorLog /var/log/apache/staticred-error.log
    CustomLog /var/log/apache/staticred-access.log combined
    <Directory /home/staticred/public_html>
        Options Indexes Includes FollowSymLinks MultiViews
        AllowOverride All
    </Directory>
    <Directory /home/staticred/public_html/mt>
        Options Indexes Includes FollowSymLinks ExecCGI MultiViews
        AllowOverride All
    </Directory>
    ScriptAlias /cgi-bin/ /home/staticred/public_html/cgi-bin/
    <Directory /home/staticred/public_html/cgi-bin>
        Options Indexes Includes FollowSymLinks MultiViews ExecCGI
        AllowOverride All
    </Directory>
</VirtualHost>
```

It's important to note the following directives:

- NameVirtualHost
- VirtualHost
- ServerAdmin
- DocumentRoot
- ServerName
- ServerAlias
- ErrorLog
- CustomLog
- ScriptAlias

\<VirtualHost\>

The \<VirtualHost\> directive tells Apache that the configuration contained within it is referring to a secondary domain on the server, rather than the primary domain. It takes two parameters: the IP address of the domain and the port. The syntax is as follows:

```
<VirtualHost 11.22.33.44:port>
```

More often than not, you'll see only the IP address on the server. Occasionally, however, a single server may have more than one IP address assigned to it, so you need to specify the correct IP address. An example is given in the Apache documentation, where the server is to be made available on both the intranet (where it has an IP address of 192.168.1.2) and the Internet (where it has an IP address of 204.255.176.199). The \<VirtualHost\> directive would look like this:

```
<VirtualHost 192.168.0.2 204.255.176.199>
```

Although the IP address isn't required in the configuration, it's a very good idea to include it. This will save Apache some time in recognizing the domain name, because it won't have to ask the DNS server to look it up.

As I mentioned before, you can also specify the port if you aren't running Apache on the standard port (80). The directive used to configure Apache to use port 8080 would be as follows:

```
<VirtualHost 204.255.176.199:8080>
```

You can also include the following above the \<VirtualHost\> directive to perform the same function:

```
Listen 204.255.176.199:8080
```

ServerAdmin

This is identical to the ServerAdmin directive used in the primary domain's configuration. However, in the context of virtual hosting, the ServerAdmin directive should be changed to point to the email address of the person looking after the domain. This way, any troubles with the domain will be emailed directly to them.

The syntax of the ServerAdmin directive is as follows:

```
ServerAdmin user@host.com
```

DocumentRoot

The DocumentRoot directive works exactly like it does in the primary domain's configuration, but will point to the public html directory of your domain's primary user instead of the primary domain's main directory. In the case of staticred.net, this would point to /var/home/staticred.net/public_html/. It's a good idea to separate the document root directories for different domains so that you can avoid confusion. Mimicking the user hierarchy is a good way of managing things.

Under Windows, it's a good idea to create a C:\htdocs folder and place each subdomain within it. For example, the staticred.net domain would be in C:\htdocs\staticred.net\, and the staticred.com domain would be in C:\htdocs\staticred.com\. By default, Apache installs the htdocs directory within its directory in the Program Files folder.

The syntax is as follows:

```
DocumentRoot </path/to/directory>
```

ServerName and ServerAlias

Here's where the actual domain configuration comes in. The ServerName directive takes a single parameter—the domain name. It looks something like this:

```
ServerName staticred.net
```

After you've declared the primary domain name for the virtual host, you can now set up aliases for it. The most common one, of course, is www. You could also set up ww.staticred.net or wwww.staticred.net (common type of subdomains). You could even go wild and set up a.little.bit.of.staticred.net.

ServerAlias is also useful so that you can point completely different domain names to the same DocumentRoot without having to duplicate configurations. For example, you could register two domains—domaina.com and domainz.com—and set domaina.com up in the ServerName directive and domainz.com in the ServerAlias directive. No matter which one of the domains a browser requested, the same content would be sent back. This is the secret trick of the bulk domain registry sites: parking thousands of domains on their servers.

The syntax of the ServerAlias directive is as follows:

```
ServerAlias <subdomain.domain.com>
```

ErrorLog and CustomLog

The ErrorLog and CustomLog directives are used to set up individual log files for each domain. I'd highly recommend this practice, because it makes things such as statistical analysis and archiving much easier in the long run. The ErrorLog directive stores Apache runtime information; the CustomLog stores the activity between Apache and its web clients.

The syntax for the ErrorLog and CustomLog directives is as follows:

```
ErrorLog /path/to/error.log
CustomLog /path/to/access.log type
```

The ErrorLog directive is relatively straightforward: You need only point it to the location of the domain's error.log file. The CustomLog directive takes an additional parameter, which tells it which type of access log to record. You can find more information on this in Chapter 8.

ScriptAlias

The ScriptAlias directive in the Virtual Host configuration is identical to the one in the main domain configuration. However, you'll want to point the ScriptAlias to a unique directory for every domain. In this way, you can keep scripts separate from one domain to another, and avoid conflicting scripts from one domain to another.

The first parameter of the ScriptAlias directive sets up the name of the CGI directory, as Apache will see it, and is relative to the DocumentRoot. The second parameter points to the physical location of the scripts directory.

One of the most best reasons for using the ScriptAlias directive is to be able to use CGI scripts that live outside of your DocumentRoot directory. For example, say you have two domains whose DocumentRoot directives point to different folders, but you want to share CGI scripts between two of them. By using the ScriptAlias directive, you can place the CGI scripts within the DocumentRoot for the first domain, then point the second domain's ScriptAlias to that folder; it will appear as though the folder exists on both domains.

The syntax for the ScriptAlias directive is as follows:

```
ScriptAlias /cgi-bin/ /home/staticred/public_html/cgi-bin/
```

Using separate configuration files

A great way to maintain your virtual hosts is to separate them into individual configuration files. By using individual configuration files, you can quickly find and make changes to a domain's directives. In addition, you can give control of the domain configuration to individual users on the system without compromising the other domains or the main Apache configuration. As far as Apache's concerned, it's as though you included the information into the main httpd.conf.

To import files into the httpd.conf, you can make use of the Include directive. The include directive takes the following syntax:

```
Include /etc/apache/virtualhost.conf
```

The best practice to use with the Include directive is to specify the file's absolute physical path. However, you can also specify paths relative to the Apache ServerRoot directory. The same file (assuming the ServerRoot were set to /etc/apache) would be as follows:

```
Include virtualhost.conf
```

Once you've separated the configuration into individual files, you can give read and write permissions to allow users to make modifications to their domain information.

I'll explore using separate configuration files in more detail in Chapter 9.

4

Summing it up

Let's review: In order to configure virtual hosts, you need to first configure their DNS settings. Ideally, you'll find someone else to do this for you. If you have to do it yourself, use the examples at the start of this chapter, and change them to suit your domain. Better yet, install one of the many DNS maintenance utilities, such as DeEnesse or Webmin.

Once your DNS configuration is set, you can move on to configure Apache for the virtual hosts running on the server. These configurations can be placed within the main httpd.conf configuration file, or included as separate configuration files within the httpd.conf configuration file. Once your virtual hosts are configured, restart Apache and test them out.

In the next chapter, I'll discuss modules. I've already touched on this, but I'll go into it in much greater detail in Chapter 5.

5 MODULES

In this chapter, I'm going to discuss the following:

- What modules are, and why they're important
- What modules are installed by default
- Where to find additional modules
- How to install modules
- Recommended modules

One of the reasons Apache is such a lean server application is that its many directives are broken out into a modular system that breaks functionality into several library files. These files are only accessed when Apache needs them, which means Apache doesn't have to store the information in memory until it's needed. These libraries are called (surprise) modules in Apache.

Apache comes with a wide variety of modules, including virtual hosting, authentication, CGI scripting, and URL rewriting. By default quite a few modules are enabled in Apache, because they're crucial to the day-to-day operations of your website (for example, the CGI module is enabled by default in order to allow you to run CGI scripts on your web server).

Apache's modules don't really follow a set naming scheme, but seem to use one of two conventions most of the time. The most common naming convention is mod_modulename. For example, the module that governs CGI applications is named mod_cgi. Almost all of the modules developed and released by the Apache Group follow this convention.

The second most common way to name Apache modules takes its inspiration from Perl. Perl modules are often named along the lines of Application::Function. An example of this would be Apache::RandomImage (a module that randomly displays images in a directory).

For most people, the modules that are included with Apache by default are more than enough to handle a website's daily needs. In fact, the only time you should need to add modules are for scripting languages, or specific programming functionality (image manipulation libraries, for example). Apache makes use of the Perl module format, which gives it access to literally thousands of modules.

What modules are installed by default?

The modules in the following sections are installed by default in both Apache 1.3 and 2.0. In Apache 1.3, they're included in the httpd.conf file by using the AddModule directive. In Apache 2.0, they're included by using the LoadModule directive. For more information on individual directives within these modules, consult the Apache documentation.

mod_env.c

This module allows CGI scripts and Server Side Includes (SSI) commands to access Apache's environment variables, which track information such as the current client's IP address, browser, referrer, and so on.

The mod_env module contains the following directives:

- PassEnv
- SetEnv
- UnsetEnv

mod_log_config.c

This module allows for use of the CustomLog directive. See Chapter 8 for more information on configuring logging. The following directives are contained in the mod_log_config module:

- CookieLog
- CustomLog
- LogFormat
- TransferLog

mod_mime.c

This module is used to determine how certain documents are to be displayed. For example, an HTML document is displayed quite differently than a simple text document. The mod_mime module contains the following directives:

- AddCharset
- AddEncoding
- AddHandler
- AddLanguage
- AddType
- DefaultLanguage
- ForceType
- RemoveEncoding
- RemoveHandler
- RemoveType
- SetHandler
- TypesConfig

mod_negotiation.c

This module works with the MultiViews directive to find documents that match a requested file name. The mod_negotiation module contains the following directives:

- CacheNegotiatedDocs
- LanguagePriority

mod_include.c

This module enables SSI. See Chapter 6 for more information. The mod_include module contains the following directive:

- XBitHack

mod_autoindex.c

This module automatically creates an index of a requested directory if no DirectoryIndex file is set or found within the directory. The mod_autoindex module contains the following directives:

- AddAlt
- AddAltByEncoding
- AddAltByType
- AddDescription
- AddIcon
- AddIconByEncoding
- AddIconByType
- DefaultIcon
- FancyIndexing
- HeaderName
- IndexIgnore
- IndexOptions
- IndexOrderDefault
- ReadmeName

mod_dir.c

This module tells Apache what files to load automatically when a directory is requested. For example, if you configure the DirectoryIndex directive as index.html, the index.html file will be loaded when a browser requests www.domain.com/somedir/. If this isn't enabled, the browser will be presented with a file listing of all documents within the folder.

mod_isapi.c

> This module is only available for Windows.

This module allows ISAPI DLL files to be used as modules by Apache for Windows. The Apache Group doesn't create ISAPI modules, so they don't provide direct support for them.

Most Apache modules will not use ISAPI, so this shouldn't be an issue. The mod_isapi module contains the following directives:

- ISAPIReadAheadBuffer
- ISAPILogNotSupported
- ISAPIAppendLogToErrors
- ISAPIAppendLogToQuery

mod_cgi.c

This module is used by Apache to run any CGI script or any file with a MIME type of application/x-http-cgi. The mod_cgi module contains the following directives:

- ScriptLog
- ScriptLogLength
- ScriptBuffer

mod_asis.c

This module is used by Apache to send files with their own HTTP headers. It's used mostly for redirects. This module has no associated directives.

mod_imap.c

This module is used for server-side image map processing. The mod_imap module contains the following directives:

- ImapMenu
- ImapDefault
- ImapBase

mod_actions.c

This module lets you run specific CGI scripts whenever a certain file type is requested. See http://httpd.apache.org/docs/mod/mod_actions.html for more information. The mod_actions module contains the following directives:

- Action
- Script

mod_userdir.c

This module allows you to host user directories in Apache. For more information, see Chapter 2. The mod_userdir module contains the following directive:

- UserDir

mod_alias.c

This module allows you to map directories outside your DocumentRoot as part of your web documents. For example, you could create a shared cgi-bin directory at /usr/lib/cgi-bin (or C:\cgi-bin), and alias it to www.domain.com/cgi-bin. The mod_alias module contains the following directives:

- Alias
- AliasMatch
- Redirect
- RedirectMatch
- RedirectTemp
- RedirectPermanent
- ScriptAlias
- ScriptAliasMatch

mod_access.c

This module allows for access control by IP address. See Chapter 3 for more information. The mod_access module contains the following directives:

- Allow
- Deny
- Order

mod_auth.c

This module allows for username- and password-based authentication control. See Chapter 3 for more information. The mod_auth module contains the following directives:

- AuthGroupFile
- AuthUserFile
- AuthAuthoritative

mod_so.c

> *This module is only available for Apache 1.3.*

This is an experimental module that allows you to load new modules into Apache without having to recompile. Apache 2.0 has this functionality built in. The mod_so module contains the following directives:

- LoadFile
- LoadModule

mod_setenvif.c

This module allows you to set environment variables if certain criteria are met. The mod_setenvif module contains the following directives:

- BrowserMatch
- BrowserMatchNoCase
- SetEnvIf
- SetEnvIfNoCase

Where do I find modules?

As you've already seen, Apache installs almost all of the modules that you'll need. If you find yourself needing something that isn't provided by the Apache Group, there are two places where you can go.

The first is the Apache Group's documentation, which has a list of modules developed by the Apache Group and included for use with Apache. It's not a long list, but you might find what you need there. You can find the list of included modules at the following URL: http://httpd.apache.org/docs/mod/index-bytype.html.

If the list of included modules doesn't contain what you need, you can go to the Apache Group's database of third-party modules. For example, you might want an Apache module that allows you to run ASP on your Apache server. This isn't supported by any of Apache's official modules, but a third-party module is available at the following URL: www.apache-asp.org/.

How do I install modules?

If you find an Apache module that you'd like to install, it's a relatively simple process to install and configure a module.

AddModule

If you're using Apache 1.3 without the mod_so module installed, this is the only way you can add modules to the system. The AddModule directive loads precompiled modules into Apache when they're needed. A typical AddModule directive looks like this:

```
AddModule mod_mime.c
```

The downside to this directive is that modules have to be precompiled against Apache before you can use them. This means recompiling Apache every time you need to add a new module, or trying to plan ahead of time for modules you may need in the future.

If you're using Apache 2.0, or you have the mod_so module installed in Apache 1.3, make use of LoadModule instead.

LoadModule

In Apache 2.0 and Apache 1.3 with the mod_so module installed, you can make use of the LoadModule directive to dynamically load modules. The LoadModule directive doesn't require modules to be compiled against Apache ahead of time—it makes use of precompiled binary files that are distributed with the module.

The LoadModule directive takes two options. The first option gives the name of the module as it will be known to Apache. Most modules will tell you what their suggested name is in their documentation. I'd recommend sticking to their suggestions. The second option tells Apache where it can find the module's library file. In Linux and Mac OS X, this file will have an .so extension. In Windows, this file will have a .dll extension.

A typical LoadModule directive looks like this:

```
LoadModule include_module modules/mod_include.so
```

AddType

This module allows you to specify, outside of the mime.types configuration file, how Apache should handle certain file types. For example, in Chapter 6, we're going to discuss adding PHP to your server. As part of that configuration, you'll have to tell Apache how to handle files with the .php extension. Let's add a line like this:

```
AddType application/x-http-php    .php
```

Configuring the module

Many modules will have their own configuration directives that Apache won't understand if the module fails to load. As a result, it's a good idea to make use of conditional <IfModule> sections within your httpd.conf so that you can contain these; if the module doesn't load, Apache will skip them entirely.

These sections only load directives if Apache can find and load the module to which they're attached. An example of this is included in the sample httpd.conf installed with Apache:

```
<IfModule mod_ssl.c>
    Include conf/ssl.conf
</IfModule>
```

Recommended modules

In addition to the default Apache modules mentioned earlier, I'd also suggest enabling the following modules:

- mod_rewrite and mod_alias
- mod_throttle

mod_rewrite and mod_alias

You use the mod_rewrite and mod_alias modules for redirecting content within your website so that you don't have to notify or wait for user input. They're also useful for redirecting content without having to affect search-engine rankings. I covered redirecting traffic in Chapter 3, but it can't hurt to revisit it.

To enable the mod_rewrite module, you'll first need to load the module. You can do so by placing the following line in your httpd.conf configuration file:

```
LoadModule rewrite_module /usr/lib/apache/1.3/mod_rewrite.so
```

Next, you need to configure the rewrite options and create a rewrite rule. In the following example, you're going to redirect visitors from www.ufies.org/arcterex/blog/ to www.arcterex.net/blog/. Place the following within a <Directory> section in your httpd.conf configuration file:

```
<IfModule rewrite_module>
RewriteEngine On
RewriteBase /arcterex/blog/
RewriteRule ^index\.html http://www.arcterex.net/blog/
</IfModule>
```

These directives break down in the following way: First, the RewriteEngine on directive tells Apache to enable the rewrite feature. Next, the RewriteBase tells Apache which directory to look for the source file in. In this case, you only want it to look in /arcterex/blog/. Once you've established the directory that it will look in, you can go about creating a rewrite rule. In this case, you want people loading the index.html file to be redirected to www.arcterex.com/blog/.

mod_throttle

The mod_throttle module is a godsend for owners of extremely busy websites. This module allows you to control access to your server, based on the speed, the amount of data transferred, or the amount of requests allowed for each time period for sites and directories on your Apache server.

The ability to throttle traffic on your server allows you to control exactly how much information is transferred. If you have monthly bandwidth limits from your provider, this can help you stay within those limits. It can also help mitigate the effect of extremely heavy traffic periods on your server's performance.

Installing the mod_throttle module is easy, but a little scary. It's not a supplied Apache module like the mod_rewrite module. This means that you'll have to download it and compile it yourself on your Linux or Mac OS X system. To do this, download the file from www.snert.com/Software/mod_throttle/#download and extract it to a temporary directory. In this directory, type the following command:

```
make; make install
```

The module will now be installed as a Dynamic Shared Object (DSO) file available to Apache. To use the mod_throttle module, you'll have to load it into Apache. Add the following line to your httpd.conf with the other loaded modules:

```
LoadModule throttle_module /usr/lib/apache/mod_throttle.so
```

Next, jump in the httpd.conf configuration file to your main <Directory> section. Place the following inside:

```
<IfModule throttle_module>
ThrottlePolicy request 10 1s
ThrottlePolicy speed 100 1s
</IfModule>
```

This can also be used in the <VirtualHost> section for sites that use virtual hosting.

The previous directives do two things. First, they tell Apache to only take a maximum of ten requests per second. Any additional requests are denied access to the site. Second, they limit the speed of information to and from your web server to 100 KB per second. This prevents your server from going into "burst mode," which sends data by using all available bandwidth. If all available bandwidth is being used by a single connection, then nothing is left over for other connections to the server.

Summing it up

Modules are a very useful part of Apache that you should get to know. Read through the Apache documentation and learn which directives are located in which modules. Often, the documentation will tell you (for example, the AddHandler directive is part of the mod_mime module).

Next, I'm going to talk about scripting languages and Apache. I'll briefly cover Perl, PHP, and SSI, and talk about how to configure them all for use with Apache.

6 SCRIPTING LANGUAGES & SERVER SIDE INCLUDES

At some point in your life as a web developer, you're going to have to work with scripting languages and Server Side Includes (SSI). I know, it's a pain in the butt, and I resisted it as long as I could. But I eventually gave in and so will you (cue dramatic music).

It's really not as bad as it seems. I started on my journey toward scripting languages with SSI. I'd been developing websites the old old-fashioned way—by editing individual HTML documents and uploading them to the web server. It was brutal, grueling work that caused me hours of grief whenever there were any changes that needed to be made to the look and feel of a website. SSI allowed me to configure specific header and footer files and place them in a central location; this freed up my content from the presentation and made global look and feel updates quick and painless. I'll talk about it in a bit more detail later in this chapter.

After learning SSI, I eventually moved on to learn some scripting languages. SSI gave me the freedom to separate my content from its presentation; scripting languages gave me the freedom to separate my content from its source. Scripting languages give you the ability to generate content dynamically, retrieve information from and store it to a database, accept user information, and even tell you when there's something wrong with the website itself. They are a must for the modern website.

The two most commonly used scripting languages for the Web are Perl and PHP.

Perl has been around for a very long time and is a very robust language. In fact, many of the modules used by Apache are themselves written in or for Perl. Because it has been around for so long, it has gained a solid reputation among web developers as a reliable, stable, and fast language.

PHP hasn't been around quite as long as Perl, but it has gained a very strong reputation over the last few years as being a robust, easy-to-use scripting language. One of the major differences between PHP and Perl is its accessibility. Perl, although extremely powerful, is often a very cryptic language—and the more advanced you get with Perl, the more cryptic the language gets. In fact, it's a badge of pride for many Perl programmers. PHP, on the other hand, is accessible for most web designers. Once you have the basics down, as far as syntax goes (if/then, for/do, and so on), the actual names of PHP functions are quite straightforward.

Not that I'm trying to sell you one solution over the other. I'll do that in another book.

Configuring Apache for Perl

You're done.

OK, perhaps it isn't quite that easy, but it almost is. You simply have to ensure that the mod_cgi module is included in your httpd.conf. The following line should be found in your modules section:

```
LoadModule cgi_module          modules/mod_cgi.so
```

You also have to ensure that Perl is installed on your server. For Linux and Mac OS X users, this isn't generally a problem. Perl is a widely used programming language, and several other applications make use of it. The chances are very good that it's already installed for you. Simply type perl -v at the command prompt. If you see the words "This is perl" followed by a version number and some copyright information, you're in the money.

It's a little more difficult for Windows users, since Perl isn't installed by default on the Windows operating system. You'll have to find a Windows-based Perl distribution and install that. A company named ActiveState has cornered the market for Windows-based Perl with their ActivePerl product. Luckily, they provide ActivePerl free of charge. You can find ActivePerl at the following URL: www.activestate.com/Products/ActivePerl/.

Once ActivePerl is installed on your system, you'll be able to run Perl scripts on your Apache server. You can also download additional Perl modules for use with Apache from CPAN at www.cpan.org.

Configuring Apache for PHP

The PHP module isn't distributed with Apache, so you have to install it on your own. PHP offers binary installs for Mac OS X and Windows, but not for Linux systems. This isn't a huge problem, thankfully, because most Linux distributions offer PHP binaries.

Running PHP on a Windows server

> *According to the PHP Group, support for Apache 2.0 is "experimental" as of PHP 4.3.4 (the latest stable version as of the writing of this book). Install it at your own risk.*

There are two methods for running PHP in Apache under Windows: CGI or Apache module. Running it in CGI mode will call the Apache executable every time a PHP script is called on the server. Running PHP as an Apache module makes use of a DLL file that mimics the PHP executable.

At the moment, installing PHP under Windows is a choice between two evils. Running PHP in CGI mode offers stability, but has the possibility of being less secure overall. Running PHP as an Apache module offers much better security, but is less stable at the moment, since it's relatively new to the PHP code base. The PHP Group recommends using the Apache module, so let's stick with that.

Installing PHP as an Apache module under Windows

> *The full guide to installing PHP under Apache can be found at www.umesd.k12.or.us/php/win32install.html, or in the install.txt file within the PHP zip package.*

The following is a summary of the install.txt file:

1. Download the PHP zip package from http://ca.php.net/downloads.php. This package allows you to choose between running PHP as a CGI application and running it as an Apache module, and comes with several additional extensions that may come in handy. The installer will only install PHP as a CGI application under Apache and doesn't include additional extensions to PHP.

2. Extract the contents of the zip package to a temporary folder (let's use C:\phpsetup for this example). When you open the temporary folder, you should see a directory similar to php-4.3.4-Win32.

3. Create a new folder called C:\php, and copy the contents of the php-4.3.4-Win32 folder into it. You should now see something like this:

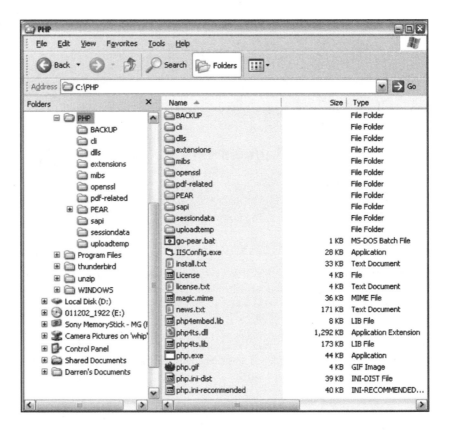

4. Open the php.ini-dist file in a text editor such as Notepad.

   A. Find the extension_dir configuration option, and change the value from ./ to the location of your PHP directory (C:\php\extensions, for example).

   B. Use the doc_root option to specify the location of Apache's DocumentRoot folder:

   doc_root = "C:\htdocs"

C. Select the extensions you'd like to enable by removing the semicolon (;) from in front of the extension. For the moment, you can likely leave all of these disabled, since the two important ones, MySQL and ODBC, are built into PHP.

D. Find the [mail function] section and configure the SMTP option to point to your outgoing mail server. This will allow you to send email through scripts (required for contact forms and useful for sending debug and error information).

E. Find the [MySQL] section, and configure your MySQL options here. One of the useful parts of this configuration section is that you can specify a default host, username, and password for your MySQL server. If you don't specify these in the php.ini file, you'll have to include them in your scripts, thereby adding a potential for security breach.

F. Save the file as php.ini.

5. Copy the php.ini file from your PHP folder to your Windows folder.

6. Copy the php4ts.dll file from your PHP install folder to your Windows System32 folder.

7. Open the sapi folder. Copy the php4apache.dll file to your Windows System32 folder (C:\winnt\system32 for Windows 2000 users, and C:\windows\system32 for Windows XP users) for Apache 1.3. If you're running Apache 2.0, copy the php4apache2.dll file instead.

8. Open your httpd.conf file, and add the PHP module to the end of the LoadModule list, as follows:

```
LoadModule php4_module"C:/php/sapi/php4apache.dll"
```

If you're installing PHP under Apache 2.0, place this at the end of the LoadModule list:

```
LoadModule php4_module "C:/php/sapi/php4apache2.dll"
```

9. At the end of the AddModule list, add the following PHP module to Apache:

```
AddModule mod_php4.c
```

If you're running PHP as a CGI service under Windows, add the following:

```
ScriptAlias /php/ "C:/php/"
Action Application/x-httpd-php "/php/php.exe"
```

10. Finally, add the following section to your httpd.conf:

```
<IfModule mod_php4.c>
AddType application/x-http/php      .php
AddType application/x-http/php-source     .phps
</IfModule>
```

This section tells Apache that if the PHP module is loaded, then files with the .php extension will be executed as PHP scripts. Furthermore, files with the .phps extension will be displayed as syntax-highlighted text when they're requested by a browser.

6

Server Side Includes

If you want to learn to do more than simple HTML on your website, SSI is where you should start. A rudimentary programming language built into Apache, SSI is provided by the mod_include module.

As you may have already guessed, the primary purpose of SSI is to allow you to include files within an HTML document. Although this doesn't sound very exciting at first, it will open up a whole new world of possibility. SSI is an incredibly helpful tool for the webmaster on the go. With it you can create a single header and footer for your website, which then wraps around your content. A simple template would look something like this:

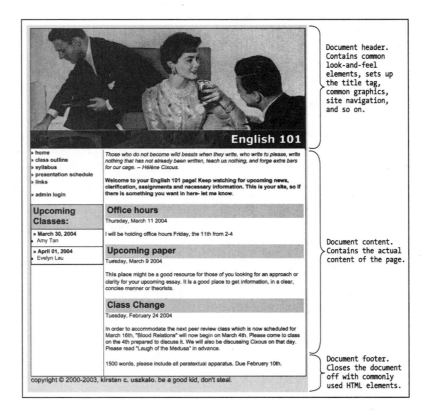

Document header. Contains common look-and-feel elements, sets up the title tag, common graphics, site navigation, and so on.

Document content. Contains the actual content of the page.

Document footer. Closes the document off with commonly used HTML elements.

Configuring Server Side Includes in Apache

To make use of SSI, the mod_include module must be enabled within the httpd.conf configuration file. In Windows installs, the mod_include module is enabled by default. However, it may not be enabled by default in some Linux installs.

The following line should be found in your httpd.conf file in Apache 1.3:

```
AddModule mod_include.c
```

If you're using Apache 2.0, the following line will be used instead:

```
LoadModule include_module modules/mod_include.so
```

Once you've enabled the module, you have to tell Apache to use includes. The first step is add a new file type and associate a handler with it. Enter the following into your httpd.conf configuration file:

```
AddType text/html .shtml
AddHandler server-parsed .shtml
```

The first line tells Apache that all files with an .shtml extension will be handled as HTML files. If this line isn't added, Apache will display files with an .shtml extension as plain text.

The second line is specific to includes; it tells Apache that files with an .shtml extension may contain SSI directives. By default, Apache doesn't look inside all files for SSI commands. If it did, the server would take a heavy hit against performance. Instead, it only looks inside files that have a specific extension.

After you've enabled the mod_includes module and set up the new extension and handler, you'll want to specify which directories and sites are allowed to use includes. In the options of the <Directory> section of the site you wish to allow includes in, add the IncludesNOEXEC option, like this:

```
<Directory /var/www>
Options Indexes IncludesNOEXEC ExecCGI MultiViews FollowSymLinks
[ other options ]
</Directory>
```

This enables SSI securely on your website, thereby allowing all SSI commands except for exec. This is important; if exec is allowed, it can possibly be used maliciously. The exec command allows users on the system to execute system commands and displays their results in HTML form. While this is most often used for things such as directory listings, it's not too far a stretch to use it to display passwords or configuration files on the server.

You may not always want to use the .shtml extension for files that include SSI commands. So what's a designer to do? You can use the X Bit Hack. The X Bit Hack was added shortly after SSI was introduced into Apache. People didn't necessarily want others to know that they were using SSI, since there are some security concerns with it. As a result, the authors of Apache added a feature that allowed users to enable SSI within files by making them executable (noted by the X flag in UNIX file permissions). To enable this option, enter the following directive into the <Directory> sections of your httpd.conf configuration file:

```
XBitHack on
```

When this directive is enabled, Apache will search through all executable files, not just files with an .shtml extension, for SSI commands.

6

SSI syntax

The syntax behind SSI is relatively simple; it looks very similar to an HTML comment tag.

Here's a sample SSI command:

```
<!--#include virtual="/includes/header.ssi"-->
```

The previous SSI command tells the web server to include the file /includes/header.ssi when building the page. By using one simple SSI call, you can stop maintaining a multitude of files for your site's presentation, and instead maintain as little as two.

How to break up your files

The best way to break up your files is to delineate where your content resides. Let's take a look at the sample code in the following example:

```
<html>
  <head>
    <title>
    Look ma, my first SSI
    </title>
  </head>
  <body>
    <table>
    <tr>
    <td>
    <p>
    This is where the text resides, the text resides, the text resides.
    </p>
    <td>
    </tr>
    </table>
  </body>
</html>
```

Here's the how you would break the content up:

```
<!-- // Header begins here -->
    <html>
    <head>
    <title>
    Look ma, my first SSI
    </title>
    </head>
    <body>
    <table>
    <tr>
    <td>
```

```
<!-- // Header ends here // -->
<!-- // Begin Content // -->
<p>
This is where the text resides, the text resides, the text resides.
</p>
<!-- // End Content // -->
<!-- // Footer begins here // -->
<td>
</tr>
</table>
</body>
</html>
<!-- // Footer ends here // -->
```

Initially, you may want to make these same comments within your HTML files. I still find it helpful to include markers like this when designing web pages, so that I can better plan how I'll break apart files.

Before you start breaking up your files, it's a good idea to plan out the directory structure of your site. I usually create four main directories within my root web folder for my supporting files: css/, js/, includes/, and images/. Not surprisingly, css/ contains all my supporting CSS files; js/ contains my supporting JavaScript files; images/ contains all my images; and includes/ contains all my SSI files.

I also plan out fairly logical names for the files within the includes/ directory. In the following example, header.ssi will contain my header, while footer.ssi will contain my footer. An important note should be made here regarding the naming of the files: They should be given the extension .shtml (for SSI) or .asp (for ASP). If they aren't named with the proper extensions, you won't be able to use embedded commands within them. I've learned this the hard way.

Using the previous example, let's break this into its different files. Let's start with the header.ssi file. The following will be placed inside:

```
<!-- // Header begins here // -->
<html>
<head>
<title>
Look ma, my first SSI
</title>
</head>
<body>
<table>
<tr>
<td>
<!-- // Header ends here // -->
```

Next comes the footer.ssi. The following will go inside:

```
<!-- // Footer begins here // -->
<td>
</tr>
</table>
</body>
</html>
<!-- // Footer ends here // -->
```

That's the basic template. The header information is stored in header.ssi, and the footer information is saved in footer.ssi, and both of these files are placed in your /includes directory. Now how do you actually go about using these files?

In your main web folder, create a file called index.shtml. Notice the different extension on that file: .shtml. This tells Apache that the file contains SSI directives; without that extension, Apache won't bother reading the file to see if there are any SSI directives in it.

The index.shtml file will contain the following:

```
<!--#include virtual="/includes/header.ssi'-->
<!-- // Begin Content // -->
<p>
This is where the text resides, the text resides, the text resides.
</p>
<!-- // End Content // -->
<!--#include virtual="/includes/footer.ssi" -->
```

As you can see, I'm using the #include command within SSI to include the files. The #include command actually has two methods of including files: virtual and file. In most cases, you'll want to make use of the virtual method, rather than the file method, as it's easier to include files this way. The location of the files is determined relative to your main web directory, so to access your includes/header.shtml file, you simply enter virtual="/includes/header.shtml".

The #include command has two possible options: file or virtual. The file option is used to specify a file at an absolute location; for example, if you wanted to load a file called stats.html within the current directory, you would use the following command:

```
<!--#include file="stats.html"-->
```

The virtual option is used to load a file based on its location as seen from the web server. For example, if you wanted to include a file that would normally be accessed at www.domain.com/about/contacts/names.html, you would use the following command:

```
<!--#include virtual="/about/contacts/names.html"-->
```

When should you use one and not the other? It really doesn't matter, though I prefer the use of the virtual option to make files more portable. If you're always referring, as in the previous example, to /about/contacts/names.html, it doesn't matter where the actual file calling the SSI command lives.

Additional SSI commands

SSI can be used for more than including files; you can also use SSI directives to condition-ally include files, execute commands, or echo information into your document, as the following table shows.

SSI command	What it does	Sample usage
config	Controls how information is parsed. There are three options available to configure:	`<!--#config errmsg="SSI Command failed."-->` `<!--#config sizefmt="bytes"-->`
	errmsg: Configures the error message sent command fails.	
	sizefmt: Sets the file format to the browser if an SSI used when displaying a file's size using the fsize command. Takes bytes or abbrev as options (abbrev reports the file size in KB or MB).	
	timefmt: Configures how time will be displayed by SSI commands such as flastmod.	
	For more information on setting time format, consult the following URL: http://unixhelp.ed.ac.uk/ CGI/man-cgi?strftime+3.	
echo	The echo command takes the value of a variable (created using the set command), and displays it within an HTML document.	`<!--#echo var="foo"-->`

(Continued)

SSI command	What it does	Sample usage
exec	The exec command executes a script or a command on the system, then displays the result within the HTML document. There are two options: **Cgi**: Executes a CGI file. **Cmd**: Executes a system command. Note: It's recommended that you don't use the exec command, since it can potentially be used to run *any* system command.	`<!--#exec cgi="/cgi-bin/stats.cgi"-->` `<!--#exec cmd="ls -al"-->`
fsize	The fsize command displays the size of a specific file within the HTML document. The fsize command takes the same options as the include command: file="file" or virtual="/path/to/file".	`<!--#fsize virtual="/css/site.css"-->`
flastmod	The flastmod command displays the last modified time for the specified file. It takes the same options as the include command.	`<!--#flastmod file="index.html"-->`
printenv	The printenv command will display all Apache's environment variables and their contents. Though it isn't something you'd use every day, it's really handy for debugging scripts.	`<!--#printenv-->`

(Continued)

SSI command	What it does	Sample usage
set	The set command allows you to create and place values within a variable. This command is best used in concert with the echo command. It takes two options: **var**: The name of the variable. **value**: The value of the variable.	`<!--#set var="foo" value="bar"-->`

For more information on SSI, refer to Apache's tutorial site at http://httpd.apache.org/docs/howto/ssi.html.

6

Summing it up

Scripting languages are an important part of running a modern web server. Regardless of whether it will be you writing the PHP, Perl, or SSI code, it's highly likely that you will need to configure one or all of the previous languages for use in Apache.

In the next chapter, you're going to dive right into one of the most difficult parts of Apache to configure: Secure Sockets Layer (SSL) (Secure Web). It might be a good time to place a bookmark here, set the book down, and go grab some coffee. I'll wait.

7 SECURE WEB (SECURE SOCKETS LAYER)

In this chapter, I'll cover the following:

- What SSL is and why you might want to use it
- Installing the OpenSSL libraries
- What certificates are and how to install them
- Becoming your own Certificate Authority (CA)
- Configuring Apache for SSL

What is Secure Sockets Layer?

SSL is a protocol for encrypting traffic between a web server and a web browser. It's actually used for much more than just serving websites securely; you can use it to protect confidential email and to secure FTP sessions over the Internet, and you can apply it to virtually any other kind of Internet communications. It's basically an extremely complicated, number-driven form of pig Latin.

SSL was developed by Netscape in 1994 to solve a distinct problem. People were discovering that the Web wasn't nearly as secure as they'd hoped it would be. People wanted to use the Internet for something other than mindless entertainment and email joke lists (it's true!). They wanted to start using it for selling merchandise, creating employee-only sites, and making financial transactions. It was immediately clear that standard HTTP wouldn't cut it, since all the data traveled on plain text. People needed a secure way to transfer information between the browser and the server.

Several developers came up with solutions for the problem. Since Netscape had the lion's share of the market, however, their solution won out. Netscape wanted to make SSL as seamless as possible for the user—beyond giving them a notice that they were about to enter a secure connection, Netscape developers felt that the user shouldn't have to do anything. They've pretty much achieved that goal—people use SSL every day without even thinking about it.

Unfortunately, if you want to configure Apache to support SSL, you *do* have to think about it. So let's move on.

There are three SSL strengths in common use as of the writing of this book: 40 bit, 56 bit, and 128 bit. The rule of thumb is this: the higher the bit-count, the stronger the encryption is going to be, and therefore, the longer it will take someone to break the code.

To give you an idea of the difference, look at the article at www.cherry-web-hosting.com.au/hosting-faq/answers/how-secure-is-ssl.html. It shows how many possible key combinations can be made at the different key strengths.

40-bit encryption creates 1,000,000,000,000 possible keys.

56-bit encryption creates approximately 71,892,000,000,000,000 possible keys.

Finally, 128-bit encryption creates approximately 339,000,000,000,000,000,000,000,000,000,000,000,000 possible keys. Given current processor speeds, the likelihood of someone breaking 128-bit encryption within their lifetime is extremely minimal.

SSL runs as a separately configured server under Apache, similar to virtual hosts. In fact, many of the directives used for virtual hosts are employed when you configure your secure server. One difference, however, is that a secure server runs on a different port than a regular web server; secure HTTP runs on port 443, whereas regular HTTP runs on port 80.

If you haven't already read Chapter 4, I'd suggest going back and doing so before continuing.

A note before we go any further

OK, before I go any further, I should tell you that I **strongly** recommend that you avoid using Windows for your secure server. There are more than a few reasons for this, but first and foremost is the aspect of security.

A Linux server is going to provide you with much more security than a Windows server out of the box. With SSL especially, you don't want your configuration files and private keys to fall into the hands of unauthorized users. On a Linux server, these files are protected by default, since nobody without root privileges will be able to access or read the certificate and Certificate Authority (CA) files. A Mac OS X server will give you similar protection; permissions are in place to protect the files from the prying eyes of the general public.

Windows servers use a far more open security model in their default installs, whereby users on the same physical server have read rights to the entire hard drive by default. In theory, you *can* get Windows to a state in which it's nearly as secure as other servers, as far as the file system goes, but the time and sweat involved just isn't worth it.

Another strike against running a secure server on Windows is the amount of effort needed just to install the mod_ssl module. Unlike Linux and Mac OS X, which include the mod_ssl module, Windows users must download the raw source code, as well as a C compiler, then compile the source code to get the binaries. Apache doesn't include SSL support in its Windows binaries due to U.S. export regulations on encryption (don't ask). It's actually quicker and easier to install a Linux distribution such as Debian or SUSE.

Also—and this is very important—you need to have a separate IP address for your secure server. Although SSL's configuration within the httpd.conf configuration file is very similar to the virtual-host settings, a secure server needs to reserve a single IP address to verify its identity. If a secure server is set up as a virtual host, the browser will receive the wrong domain name when it attempts to verify that the IP address matches the domain name, since the IP address will only return the primary domain for which it's configured.

7

Where do I get SSL?

The SSL package most used with Apache is OpenSSL, an open-source project that is free for both commercial and noncommercial use. If you're extremely security conscious, you can visit their website at www.openssl.org, download the source code, and compile it yourself.

If you're installing a secure server on Mac OS X, then you have it made. OS X includes OpenSSL as part of the operating system. The folks at Apple really outdid themselves when they put that operating system together.

For the rest of us, there are precompiled binaries available. Each distribution has its own way of adding software to the server. For example, in Debian it's as simple as typing the following as the root:

```
apt-get install openssl
```

Red Hat requires that you download the OpenSSL RPM and its dependencies, then add it via the Red Hat rpm utility. SUSE uses the YaST tool to add software. The important thing to note here is to get your OpenSSL packages from trusted sources, such as the maker of your Linux distribution. Try to avoid sites such as "j03's l337 s0ftW4rez d0wn1o4d3rz!!!!" for your security software, for example.

Windows users can download precompiled binaries of the OpenSSL libraries in order to use them without going through the whole compilation process. Although the OpenSSL group doesn't provide Windows binaries (or any binaries, for that matter) on their site, it does recommend the binaries provided by Shining Light Productions. The most recent version can be downloaded here: www.slproweb.com/products/Win32OpenSSL.html.

Certificates

A certificate is the public key used by a web server to create a secure, encrypted connection between the browser and the server. Certificates match the private and public key pairing by creating a CA, which issues certificates to individual sites. Every certificate needs to originate from a CA in order for its authenticity to be validated. The certificates used by Apache and the mod_ssl module use a standard called X.509. An X.509 certificate carries the following information within it:

- Version
- Serial number
- Signature algorithm ID
- Issuer name
- Validity period
- Subject (user) name
- Subject public key information

- Issuer unique identifier
- Subject unique identifier
- Extensions (version 3 only)
- Signature on the previous fields[1]

A certificate is essentially just a long string of random characters that's used to encrypt a message. It looks something like this:

```
-----BEGIN CERTIFICATE-----
MIICODCCAjmgAwIBAgIBADANBgkqhkiG9w0BAQQFADBVMQswCQYDVQQGEwJDQTEQ
MA4GA1UECBMHQWxiZXJ0YTERMA8GA1UEBxMIRWRtb250b24xITAfBgNVBAoTGElu
dGVybmV0IFdpZGdpdHMgUHR5IEx0ZDAeFw0wNDAxMjcwNDQOMTNaFw0wNTAxMjYw
NDQOMTNaMFUxCzAJBgNVBAYTAkNBMRAwDgYDVQQIEwdBbGJlcnRhMREwDwYDVQQH
EwhFZG1vbnRvbjEhMB8GA1UEChMYSW50ZXJuZXQgV2lkZ2l0cyBQdHkgTHRkMIGf
MA0GCSqGSIb3DQEBAQUAA4GNADCBiQKBgQC7ot5sAlIZgyFE5JrQOiWeUocdKJ5q
mv2yJQDyfrkqz7zSDU/szfmT2WRb2veVySIATWbGPmqznOvCybDO/xulaUHvwAX+
5PgFERx1Dx4by1uY76uWnVE+/epxD14WZ3mf62LuAyU98kgCZclVZI/nx1bUfWRW
jiR3Q295lqaZBwIDAQABo4GvMIGsMB0GA1UdDgQWBBSOZf9hCHLMtxl328LRZwO+
wvKF1jB9BgNVHSMEdjB0gBSOZf9hCHLMtxl328LRZwO+wvKF1qFZpFcwVTELMAkG
A1UEBhMCQOExEDAOBgNVBAgTBOFsYmVydGExETAPBgNVBAcTCEVkbW9udG9uMSEw
HwYDVQQKExhJbnRlcm5ldCBXaWRnaXRzIFBOeSBMdGSCAQAwDAYDVROTBAUwAwEB
/zANBgkqhkiG9w0BAQQFAAOBgQAzDnL7tnpRpjsMsDpt9uThvwC1xntnPqoTelNK
wDHTfWrlVyLYLCGdqjYE+mtP8NGauzvoWVmtkG/V4WWdx7ihGfBCD97lMNwqO46n
YTok6GA1TfL+HpLP+rG8iYnnW9PV/B2eqfA+KRtwjgUVHZFsobA7KZVFo4p2Y2Ie
hdQWYA==
-----END CERTIFICATE-----
```

There are several companies that offer services as "trusted" CAs. If you're going to be running an online store or a high-profile secure site, I recommend that you go to one of these companies and purchase a certificate from them. If you're setting up a secure intranet site or a vendor portal, you can be your own CA.

The mod_ssl documentation provides a really useful diagram to describe the process of setting up a secure connection, which I've given in the following figure.[2] It breaks down to this:

1. The browser (client) sends a Hello packet to the server and requests a secure connection.

2. The server acknowledges the request and sends its public server certificate.

3. If it's requested, the browser sends a certificate back. This completes a process known as the handshake. The server and client have both sent enough information to create a connection.

4. The server and client then agree on a method of encryption to use, and a secure session is initiated.

7

---

[1] See the World Wide Web Consortium at www.w3.org/PICS/DSig/X509_1_0.html.

[2] Figure caption cited from www.modssl.org/docs/2.8/ssl_intro.html.

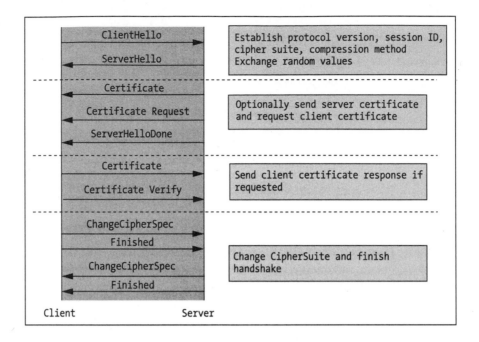

Install a certificate from a Certificate Authority

The most common type of certificate that you'll acquire will be a certificate from an established CA such as VeriSign or thawte. Both of these CAs offer 40- and 128-bit certificates for signing your website. The CA will give you two files: One is a private server key, and the other is a public server certificate. Place both of these files in your /etc/apache/ssl directory.

Installing certificates from an established CA on your web server gives you instant credibility among consumers and is pretty much necessary for online stores or other high-profile secure sites (such as financial institutions). The downside, of course, is the cost. At the time of this book's writing, VeriSign costs around $900 USD per year for a 128-bit key.

Each CA has a different process for obtaining certificates from them. Follow your CA's instructions to obtain a certificate and a key file for your server, and then skip ahead to the "Apache configuration" section.

Create a new certificate

If you want to create your own certificate, you need to set yourself up as a CA. The process is somewhat lengthy, but isn't too difficult. OpenSSL includes a utility called CA.pl to help you do it quickly and easily. However, it doesn't give you much of an idea of what's going on. So instead, I'm going to lead you through the process step by step. It will take a little longer, but it will give you a much better idea of the steps involved.

Create an RSA secure key. Don't supply a password; otherwise, Apache will wait for the password to be entered whenever you start it. Ensure that the server.key file is only readable by the root user, as follows:

```
openssl genrsa  -out server.key 1024
```

Once the server.key file is written, you must protect it from being read by anyone who isn't the root user or administrator on the system. On Linux and Mac OS X systems, you can do this through the chmod command. Type the following:

```
chmod 400 server.key
```

Generate a certificate signing request. This will be sent to the CA for signing, or be signed against your own CA, as follows:

```
openssl req -new -key server.key -out server.csr
```

In the Common Name field, enter the domain name for your secure server (that is, www.domain.com). If you supply a challenge password, the user will be asked to supply it when he installs the certificate in his browser. If no challenge password is supplied, anyone with access to the certificate will be able to use it. However, there's another important aspect of the challenge password: If you supply one, Apache will ask for it every time it restarts. If you're running a remote server, this is **not a good thing**, since Apache will just sit there, waiting for you to enter a password, and it won't load the rest of the server.

Become your own Certificate Authority

As I mentioned earlier, every certificate has to have a CA to verify its authenticity. If you can't verify the authenticity of a certificate, then the browser won't trust the connection. If you choose not to use a commercially supplied CA, you have to become your own CA.

> *End users will be notified by most browsers that the certificate that they're using doesn't come from a known CA. In order to work around this, you'll have to supply a direct link to the certificate and instruct the user to install it in their browser.*

Get started

First, you need to have a secure place to store your CA certificates and key files. On UNIX and Mac OS X systems, your best place to store these is in the /etc/ssl directory. On Windows, store them in the C:\OpenSSL\ca\ folder.

1. Create the CA directory. Under Linux, this should be stored in /etc/ssl/ca/private; in Windows, I'd suggest storing it in C:\OpenSSL\ca\private. Create the CA private keys directory as follows:

```
mkdir -p /etc/ssl/ca/private
```

2. Set the permissions of the CA directory to be readable by root or by administrator only. It's important that nobody but the root user or administrator has access to the directory that your root certificates are in; if people can access the root certificates, they can use them to decode the encrypted data between the server and a browser. Under Linux and Mac OS X, type the following at the command prompt:

```
chown -R root /etc/ssl/ca/
```

Generate the CA private key

Now that they have a place to go, you can create the key files for the CA. To do so, you need to use the openssl utility, which is supplied with the OpenSSL libraries. To start this tool, change to the directory you just created and type openssl.

```
dev:/etc/ssl# openssl
```

> *Windows users will need to specify the full path to the OpenSSL utility, which can be found at C:\OpenSSL\bin\openssl.exe.*

After you start the openssl utility, you'll be presented with an OpenSSL> prompt. Now, you can start entering commands to create your CA files. The first file you need to create is the actual key file. This file contains a random string that will be used to create your encrypted data. There are several different encryption types that you can use; RSA is the one most commonly chosen, because it's the most commonly supported among the different browser makers.

To generate an RSA key, run the genrsa command. It takes three parameters: -des3, which selects TripleDES as the encryption format; -out, which specifies the file name to write the RSA key to; and finally a bit-length for the encrypted key. The recommended bit-length is 1024. As part of the process, you'll be asked for a password for the private key. Enter a unique, hard-to-guess password for your CA private key. If anyone gains access to this password, she will be able to create new certificates using this key, thereby allowing her to successfully identify herself as your server.

```
OpenSSL> genrsa -des3 -out ca.key 1024
```

When you run the command, the utility will display the following information on the screen:

```
warning, not much extra random data, consider using the -rand option
Generating RSA private key, 1024 bit long modulus
.......................++++++
....++++++
e is 65537 (0x10001)
Enter PEM pass phrase:
Verifying password - Enter PEM pass phrase:
OpenSSL>
```

Next you have to request a new certificate from the CA through the req command. This uses the CA's private key along with some distinct information about your installation to create a unique public certificate. This command will create the public key that you'll distribute to the users of your website, and create new server certificates from.

Create a public CA certificate

The public CA certificate is used to create and sign new server certificates. This is also the file that's distributed to users of your server in order to authenticate that the server key is correct.

To create the public CA certificate, you need to use OpenSSL utility's req command. The req command takes three parameters: -new tells openssl to create a new key; -key tells it which CA key to base it on; and -out specifies the file that the certificate will be written to, as shown here:

```
OpenSSL> req -new -x509 -days 365 -key ca.key -out ca.crt
```

When run, the req command asks for some information about your installation. The following is an example of the type of information it will ask, and the sample responses. You can leave fields blank if you wish—but the more information you supply with the certificate, the more confidence the end user will have that it's secure.

```
Using configuration from /usr/lib/ssl/openssl.cnf
You are about to be asked to enter information that will be
incorporated into your certificate request.
What you are about to enter is what is called a Distinguished
Name or a DN.
There are quite a few fields but you can leave some blank
For some fields there will be a default value,
If you enter '.', the field will be left blank.
-----
Country Name (2 letter code) [AU]:CA
State or Province Name (full name) [Some-State]:Alberta
Locality Name (eg, city) []:Edmonton
Organization Name (eg, company) [Internet Widgets Pty Ltd]:Staticred
Organizational Unit Name (eg, section) []:
Common Name (eg, YOUR name) []:www.staticred.net
Email Address []:webmaster@staticred.net
OpenSSL>
```

A new key, ca.csr, will be written to the directory and you'll be returned to the OpenSSL> prompt. Before you can make use of this new public key, however, you'll have to sign it. The x509 command does this. The following command will make a new certificate (ca.crt) that expires after one year (365 days). After it expires, you'll have to generate a new CA public key. The following shows the syntax of the x509 command, and its output:

```
OpenSSL> x509 -req -days 365 -in ca.csr -signkey ca.key -out ca.crt
Signature ok
subject=/C=CA/ST=Alberta/L=Edmonton/O=StaticRed Light \
```

7

```
Industries/OU=Admin/CN=Darren James \
Harkness/Email=webmaster@staticred.net
Getting Private key
OpenSSL>
```

Sign your own certificates

In most OpenSSL distributions, a script named *sign.sh* is included. This script is used to sign new certificates from the CA. There are a couple of things you need to make sure of before running the sign.sh script:

1. Ensure that you have created a server private key and a certificate request file (server.csr). See the "Create a new certificate" section earlier.

2. Copy the server.csr file to the CA private directory (/etc/ssl/ca/private).

Once you've got everything in the right place, you can run the sign.sh script and tell it which file to sign. It looks something like this:

```
./sign.sh server.csr
```

Here's a sample of what the sign.sh script will output:

```
CA signing: server.csr -> server.crt:
Using configuration from ca.config
Check that the request matches the signature
Signature ok
The Subjects Distinguished Name is as follows
countryName          :PRINTABLE:'CA'
stateOrProvinceName  :PRINTABLE:'Alberta'
localityName         :PRINTABLE:'Edmonton'
organizationName     :PRINTABLE:'Staticred'
commonName           :PRINTABLE:'http://dev'
emailAddress         :IA5STRING:'webmaster@staticred.net'
Certificate is to be certified until Feb  1 00:49:36 2005 GMT (365
days)
Sign the certificate? [y/n]:y
1 out of 1 certificate requests certified, commit? [y/n]y
Write out database with 1 new entries
Data Base Updated
CA verifying: server.crt <-> CA cert
server.crt: OK
```

When the server.crt file has been written, you can move it and the original server.key file to /etc/apache/ssl. Ensure that the server.key file is made readable only to the root user or to the administrator. Check the "Create a new certificate" section for more information on how to do this.

The sign.sh script

If for some reason you don't have a sign.sh script, you can create it using the following code:

```
#!/bin/sh
##
##  sign.sh -- Sign a SSL Certificate Request (CSR)
##  Copyright (c) 1998-2001 Ralf S. Engelschall, All Rights Reserved.
##

#   argument line handling
CSR=$1
if [ $# -ne 1 ]; then
    echo "Usage: sign.sign <whatever>.csr"; exit 1
fi
if [ ! -f $CSR ]; then
    echo "CSR not found: $CSR"; exit 1
fi
case $CSR in
   *.csr ) CERT="`echo $CSR | sed -e 's/\.csr/.crt/'`" ;;
      * ) CERT="$CSR.crt" ;;
esac

#   make sure environment exists
if [ ! -d ca.db.certs ]; then
    mkdir ca.db.certs
fi
if [ ! -f ca.db.serial ]; then
    echo '01' >ca.db.serial
fi
if [ ! -f ca.db.index ]; then
    cp /dev/null ca.db.index
fi

#   create an own SSLeay config
cat >ca.config <<EOT
[ ca ]
default_ca              = CA_own
[ CA_own ]
dir                     = .
certs                   = \$dir
new_certs_dir           = \$dir/ca.db.certs
database                = \$dir/ca.db.index
serial                  = \$dir/ca.db.serial
RANDFILE                = \$dir/ca.db.rand
certificate             = \$dir/ca.crt
private_key             = \$dir/ca.key
default_days            = 365
default_crl_days        = 30
default_md              = md5
preserve                = no
policy                  = policy_anything
[ policy_anything ]
```

```
countryName                = optional
stateOrProvinceName        = optional
localityName               = optional
organizationName           = optional
organizationalUnitName     = optional
commonName                 = supplied
emailAddress               = optional
EOT

#  sign the certificate
echo "CA signing: $CSR -> $CERT:"
openssl ca -config ca.config -out $CERT -infiles $CSR
echo "CA verifying: $CERT <-> CA cert"
openssl verify -CAfile ca.crt $CERT

#  cleanup after SSLeay
rm -f ca.config
rm -f ca.db.serial.old
rm -f ca.db.index.old

#  die gracefully
exit 0
```

Apache configuration

Now that your server.key and server.crt files are in your /etc/apache/ssl directory, you can configure Apache to use them. There are a few steps to this:

1. Load the SSL module.

2. Configure the global SSL options.

3. Configure the specific server options.

The next sections will walk you through the final steps to getting an SSL server up and running.

Create a separate configuration file

I'd suggest creating a separate configuration file for your SSL settings and naming it ssl.conf. This file will contain all the directives and <Directory> statements for your SSL server. By keeping this file separate, you can make changes to it easily, without having to scour through your main httpd.conf to find the relevant sections.

Load the SSL module

Obviously, before you can make use of SSL, you need to ensure that the mod_ssl module is loaded. This is done through two lines in your ssl.conf:

```
LoadModule ssl_module /usr/lib/apache/1.3/mod_ssl.so
AddModule mod_ssl.c
```

Mac users will find the module located at libexec/httpd/libssl.so. Windows users will find it at modules/ssl/mod_ssl.so.

The LoadModule directive tells the Apache server what the name of the module is, and where it can find the files for it. Under a Linux system, this will be found in /usr/lib/apache/1.3 (or 2.0 for Apache 2.0 users). Under a Windows system, you can find these files in the libs folder within your Apache program directory. Once the module is loaded, you need to add the module to the server. Use the AddModule directive to do so.

Configure the SSL server

Once you've loaded the module, you can start configuring it for use in Apache.

Using IfDefine and IfModule sections

It's a good idea to include your configuration in IfDefine and IfModule sections. This way, if anything happens to go wrong with the SSL module, Apache will continue to load the rest of its configuration and ignore the SSL directives.

IfDefine sections are used to make configuration changes only when a condition is true. In this case, you want to set some directives if SSL is enabled on your server. You'll mark these sections as the following in your httpd.conf:

```
<IfDefine SSL>
[ ... set of directives ... ]
</IfDefine>
```

IfModule is similar to IfDefine, but it's used to make configuration changes only if a module exists. The IfModule section takes the module file name as its parameter. This file almost always ends with a .c extension.

You're going to use this to contain a set of directives pertaining to the SSL server. It will look like this:

```
<IfModule mod_ssl.c>
[ ... set of directives ... ]
</IfModule>
```

Look at the end of this chapter for the proper use of the IfDefine and IfModule sections.

Configure the global options

First, you need to set up some default directives for the Apache server at large.

The first directive is SSLMutex. This directive configures the SSL lockfile, which stores session data used by Apache with regards to its operations. If you aren't using session data with your SSL server, then you can leave this unconfigured.

There are three ways to configure this directive, but only one that's useful for UNIX, Windows, and Mac users: sem, as shown here:

```
SSLMutex sem
```

If for some reason sem doesn't work on your system, you can specify a location for the lockfile by using the file option. This would look something like this:

```
SSLMutex file:/var/log/apache/ssl_mutex
```

Next, you need to start the random seed generator through the SSLRandomSeed directive; this, combined with the certificate, ensures that the key used to encrypt a session isn't generated using a predictable number. There are two parameters passed to the SSLRandomSeed directive: method and context.

There are several different methods available with the SSLRandomSeed directive, but really only two that you'll make use of: builtin and file. The builtin method makes use of Apache's internal pseudo-random number generator. The upside of this is that it doesn't take any additional processor power away from your server. The downside is that it isn't as secure as other methods. Windows users will want to make use of this method, since no random device exists on a Windows server.

The file: method is available to UNIX servers, but not Windows users, and it makes use of the /dev/random or /dev/urandom devices. These devices are included with most UNIX servers and exist solely to generate random data. Since they're part of the operating system, neither of these devices take extra processor time to run. If you add a number after the file: method, this will limit the amount of data returned from the random device.

Two contexts are available for the SSLRandomSeed directive: startup and connect. The startup context starts the random generator when Apache starts; the connect context starts it when an SSL connection is initiated.

More than one SSLRandomSeed directive can be configured—and in fact, this is recommended, as follows:

```
SSLRandomSeed startup builtin
SSLRandomSeed startup file:/dev/urandom 1024
SSLRandomSeed connect file:/dev/urandom 1024
```

Next, you need to tell Apache how to deal with its session cache. By default, SSL already handles its own session cache. However, if you're running an extremely busy site, you may notice some performance issues with the default session cache. The mod_ssl documentation says that the SSLSessionCache directive is really useful when parallel requests are made—that is, when requests for a page and the graphics within it are made. The default value for this is

```
SSLSessionCache none
```

If you find that your server is experiencing performance issues, then you may want to enable the SSLSessionCache. There are two options you can use: dbm and shm. The dbm option is the recommended option in the mod_ssl documentation, and promises a noticeable speed increase. The shm option gives an even higher performance increase, as it stores the session data to a configured amount of RAM instead of to disk. However, it isn't supported by every operating system, so you may not be able to make use of it.

If you do decide to enable SSLSessionCache, you would use the following syntax:

```
SSLSessionCache dbm:/var/log/apache/ssl_cache
SSLSessionCache shm:/var/log/apache/ssl_cach(256000)
```

Finally, you need to tell Apache where to save its log data for secure connections. This is identical to the ErrorLog configuration I discussed in Chapter 4.

```
SSLLog /var/logs/apache/ssl.log
SSLLogLevel info
```

Also in Chapter 8 I talked about configuring custom access logs. When the mod_ssl module is installed on your server, you can extend custom access logs to SSL. The following log records the time, the remote host, the SSL protocol, the HTTP protocol and file requested, and finally the amount of data transferred.

```
CustomLog logs/ssl_request "%h %t %{SSL_PROTOCOL}x %{SSL_CIPHER}x
\"%r\" %b"
```

An actual entry might look something like this:

```
r334.router.domainhost.com [26/Feb/2004:23:43:22 -0700] SSLv3
ALL:!ADH:RC4+RSA:+HIGH:+MEDIUM:+LOW:+SSLv2:+EXP
"GET /index.html HTTP/1.0" 4042
```

The mod_ssl module adds the ability to use a set of preconfigured server variables, which are outlined in the following table.[3] These server variables are useful if you decide to create scripts to interact with your secure site.

Server variable	Variable type	What it holds
HTTPS	flag	true if HTTPS is being used
SSL_PROTOCOL	String	The SSL protocol version
SSL_SESSION_ID	string	The hex-encoded SSL session ID
SSL_CIPHER	string	The cipher specification name
SSL_CIPHER_EXPORT	string	true if cipher is an export cipher
SSL_CIPHER_USEKEYSIZE	number	Number of cipher bits (actually used)

(Continued)

[3] Table cited from www.modssl.org/docs/2.8/ssl_reference.html#table4.

Server variable	Variable type	What it holds
SSL_CIPHER_ALGKEYSIZE	number	Number of cipher bits (possible)
SSL_VERSION_INTERFACE	string	The mod_ssl program version
SSL_VERSION_LIBRARY	string	The OpenSSL program version
SSL_CLIENT_M_VERSION	string	The version of the client certificate
SSL_CLIENT_M_SERIAL	string	The serial of the client certificate
SSL_CLIENT_S_DN	string	Subject DN in client's certificate
SSL_CLIENT_S_DN_x509	string	Component of client's Subject DN
SSL_CLIENT_I_DN	string	Issuer DN of client's certificate
SSL_CLIENT_I_DN_x509	string	Component of client's Issuer DN
SSL_CLIENT_V_START	string	Validity of client's certificate (start time)
SSL_CLIENT_V_END	string	Validity of client's certificate (end time)
SSL_CLIENT_A_SIG	string	Algorithm used for the signature of client's certificate
SSL_CLIENT_A_KEY	string	Algorithm used for the public key of client's certificate
SSL_CLIENT_CERT	string	PEM-encoded client certificate
SSL_CLIENT_CERT_CHAINn	string	PEM-encoded certificates in client certificate chain
SSL_CLIENT_VERIFY	string	NONE, SUCCESS, GENEROUS, or FAILED:*reason*
SSL_SERVER_M_VERSION	string	The version of the server certificate
SSL_SERVER_M_SERIAL	string	The serial of the server certificate
SSL_SERVER_S_DN	string	Subject DN in server's certificate

(Continued)

Server variable	Variable type	What it holds
SSL_SERVER_S_DN_x509†	string	Component of server's Subject DN
SSL_SERVER_I_DN	string	Issuer DN of server's certificate
SSL_SERVER_I_DN_x509†	string	Component of server's Issuer DN
SSL_SERVER_V_START	string	Validity of server's certificate (start time)
SSL_SERVER_V_END	string	Validity of server's certificate (end time)
SSL_SERVER_A_SIG	string	Algorithm used for the signature of server's certificate
SSL_SERVER_A_KEY	string	Algorithm used for the public key of server's certificate
SSL_SERVER_CERT	string	PEM-encoded server certificate

† where x509 is a component of an X.509 DN: C,ST,L,O,OU,CN,T,I,G,S,D,UID,Email

Configure the secure server

Now that you have the global SSL settings, you need to tell Apache about the SSL server itself. This follows the form of a virtual host; in fact, Apache makes complete use of its virtual-host functionality to configure SSL, and all directives used for virtual hosts are available for SSL servers. One difference, however, is that SSL-specific directives are included in the <VirtualHost> section. At its basic, least-configured state, you should include the following information:

```
<VirtualHost www.my-server.dom:443>
SSLEngine On
SSLcertificateFile /etc/apache/ssl/server.crt
SSLcertificateKeyFile /etc/apache/ssl/server.key
</VirtualHost>
```

The SSLEngine directive turns the SSL module on for this site; without this option set, you don't have a secure server. So don't forget this directive!

Next, you need to tell Apache where the certificate and certificate key files are. The SSLcertificateFile directive tells the server where the public certificate file is located. Earlier you obtained these files from either an existing CA, or by becoming your own CA, and you placed them in the /etc/apache/ssl directory.

7

In the end, your ssl.conf configuration file should look like this:

```
# SSL Configuration File - ssl.conf
LoadModule ssl_module /usr/lib/apache/1.3/mod_ssl.so
AddModule mod_ssl.c
SSLMutex sem
SSLRandomSeed startup builtin
SSLRandomSeed startup file:/dev/urandom 1024
SSLRandomSeed connect file:/dev/urandom 1024
SSLSessionCache none
SSLLog /var/logs/apache/ssl.log
SSLLogLevel info
CustomLog logs/ssl_request "%t %h %{SSL_PROTOCOL}x %{SSL_CIPHER}x
\"%r\" %b"
<VirtualHost www.my-server.dom:443>
SSLEngine On
SSLcertificateFile /etc/apache/ssl/server.crt
SSLcertificateKeyFile /etc/apache/ssl/server.key
</VirtualHost>
<IfDefine SSL>
  AddType application/x-x509-ca-cert .crt
  AddType application/x-pkcs7-crl    .crl
  </IfDefine>
  <IfModule mod_ssl.c>
  SSLPassPhraseDialog  builtin
  SSLSessionCache     dbm:/apache/var/logs/ssl_scache
  SSLSessionCacheTimeout  300
  SSLMutex  file:/apache/var/logs/ssl_mutex
  SSLRandomSeed startup builtin
  SSLRandomSeed connect builtin
  SSLLog      /apache/var/logs/ssl_engine_log
  SSLLogLevel info
  </IfModule>
 <IfDefine SSL>
  <VirtualHost _default_:443>
  DocumentRoot "/apache/htdocs"
  ServerName ns.mynet.home
  ServerAdmin asis@ns.mynet.home
  ErrorLog /apache/var/logs/error_log
  TransferLog /apache/var/logs/access_log
  SSLEngine on
  SSLCipherSuite ALL:!ADH:!EXP56:RC4+RSA:+HIGH:+MEDIUM:+LOW:
➥+SSLv2:+EXP:+eNULL
  SSLCertificateFile /apache/conf/server.crt
  SSLCertificateKeyFile /apache/conf/server.key
  <Files ~ "\.(cgi|shtml|phtml|php3?)$">
      SSLOptions +StdEnvVars
  </Files>
  <Directory "/apache/cgi-bin">
```

```
        SSLOptions +StdEnvVars
    </Directory>
    SetEnvIf User-Agent ".*MSIE.*" \
            nokeepalive ssl-unclean-shutdown \
            downgrade-1.0 force-response-1.0
    CustomLog /apache/var/logs/ssl_request_log \
            "%t %h %{SSL_PROTOCOL}x %{SSL_CIPHER}x \"%r\" %b"
    </VirtualHost>
    </IfDefine>
```

Secure Sockets Layer or Transport Layer Security?

There are actually three methods of encryption that you can use with Apache's secure server: SSLv2, SSLv3, and TLS.

SSLv2 is the predecessor to SSLv3, and doesn't offer the same level of encryption and security as SSLv3. If you have a choice, always go with SSLv3, since it's more secure. If you know for a fact, however, that you need to support a web browser that isn't compatible with SSLv3, then you should set up a server using this level of encryption instead. If you need to create an SSLv2-only server, place the following lines into the global section of your ssl.conf configuration file, as follows:

```
SSLProtocol -all +SSLv2
SSLCipherSuite SSLv2:+HIGH:+MEDIUM:+LOW:+EXP
```

TLS is the successor to SSLv3 and definitely offers a few improvements on SSL's security model. There's only one catch—support is reportedly a little sketchy. Though most of the major browsers support TLS, it seems to be disabled by default in most of them. As a result, unless you can guarantee that the browsers connecting to your website are configured to use TSL, you should set your site up to use SSLv3. Eventually, TLS is going to become a widely adopted standard and I predict that it will take over from SSL when it comes to securing websites. But for now, let's stick to SSL.

Installing a Certificate Authority public key

If you're acting as your own CA, you'll need to distribute your CA public key (ca.crt) to users on your website. Any time a browser first connects to a secure server that's acting as its own CA, the browser will warn the user and ask him if it's OK to connect. By providing the CA public key on your website, users can install the public key in their browser, thereby automatically making it a trusted source of information (and hence not getting the warning any longer).

Create a directory in your document root directory. For example, if your document root directory was /var/www, you'd copy the ca.crt file there. You could also create a cert/ directory within /var/www to keep things clean. Once copied to the document root directory, you'll need to add a link to it within the HTML of your site.

Each browser handles certificates differently. In Internet Explorer, the certificate's details will be displayed, along with an Install Certificate button, as shown in the following figure:

Once you click the Install Certificate button, IE will lead you through an import wizard. Simply follow the directions on the screen.

Mozilla handles this differently. After you click the public CA certificate, it asks you what you want to do with it. You'll see the following figure:

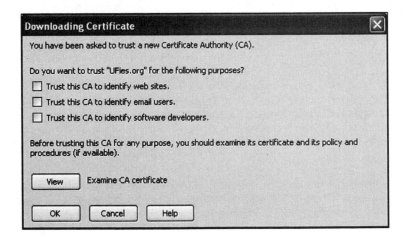

Select what level of trust you wish to associate the certificate with, and click OK.

Summing it up

Once you have your ssl.conf file configured and your server key and public certificate installed, you can restart Apache and test your secure server. Test the server by loading it up using the https:// prefix. For example, if your server existed at http://www.domain.com, you would load the secure server by loading https://www.domain.com in your browser. If everything worked correctly, you should see your page and an icon indicating that you're connected to a secure server.

In the next chapter, I'll discuss Apache's log files, how to configure them, and why they're useful.

7

8 LOG FILES

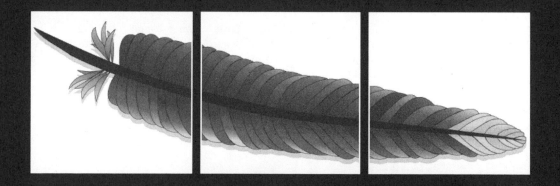

In previous chapters, I've talked about configuring several Apache features, but I haven't talked about the most important Apache feature that you'll use: logging. Apache supplies two types of log files that track the activities of the Apache web server, both of which range from errors encountered with the application and modules to pages requested by your website's users.

Log files are the bookkeepers of the web-server world. They're plain (text) and boring, but of essential importance to daily operations. As you start working with Apache more often and consult log files on a regular basis, you'll start—much like your bookkeeper—to grow more comfortable with them as you get used to them.

In this chapter, I'm going to introduce you to error.log and access.log, the two main log files used in Apache. I'll tell you how to configure them, and what information they'll tell you. I'll also tell you how to configure the log files for virtual hosts so that you can avoid a jumbled mess of log entries.

Before you begin

Before you begin configuring and using the Apache log files, let's take a moment to talk about security. Apache generally runs with root or administrator privileges; log files should be created with root or administrator privileges as a result.

Apache's log files contain raw data about who is accessing your site, and what errors your Apache server encounters while running. If someone has write access to the log files, he can easily add to or remove information from the logs, thereby contributing to bad data.

This does assume that they have access to the server in the first place. Of course, most security breaches on the Internet originate from within an organization. It's just best practice to cover your rear now and take steps to keep your Apache server secure. In other words, be careful with the permissions on your log directory. Don't let just anyone have access to the log files.

> Older versions of Apache don't filter the information placed in the log files in any way. It's possible that someone could insert control characters into a URL request, which would then make it into the raw log files. If viewed through a regular terminal window (by echoing the contents of the file using cat, for example), there's the potential for a malicious command to be executed on your server. This has been fixed in Apache 1.3.25 and Apache 2.0.46.

error.log

The error.log file archives all notices, warnings, and program errors encountered by Apache. Where the error.log is really useful is for CGI scripts. If an error is encountered in the CGI script, and it's written to output an error, this error will appear in the error.log verbatim. Most of the time, however, this file can be safely ignored, unless your web server is acting irrationally.

> *The error log file may also be named error_log, depending on your installation.*

A standard entry in the error.log looks like this:

```
[Fri Oct  3 06:25:11 2003] [notice] Apache/1.3.26 (Unix)
Debian GNU/Linux PHP/4.1.2 configured — resuming normal
operations
```

This line can be broken into three parts: the first part notes the time of the log entry, in this case Friday October 3, 2003 at 06:25:11; the second part indicates the log-entry level—a notice; finally, the line contains a description of what happened—in this case the server was restarted.

Configuring the error log

To configure the error log, you need to specify two things: the location of the file itself and the amount of information you want to place within it.

The first step is pretty easy—simply tell it where you want to place the error log in the httpd.conf file. There will actually already be an entry there, and for Linux, it will look something like this:

```
ErrorLog /var/log/apache/error.log
```

and it will look like this for Windows (which will be relative to the Apache installation directory):

```
ErrorLog logs\error.log
```

The next step is a little trickier. When you're configuring Apache, you can specify what level of entries to place within this log file. This table lists the log levels by way of descending importance.[1]

Log level	Description	Example
emerg	Emergencies—Apache is unusable. Anything that would cause Apache to quit unexpectedly, or not to load will be logged as an emerg-level error.	"Child cannot open lock file. Exiting"

(Continued)

---

[1] See the "Apache Core Features" page at http://httpd.apache.org/docs/mod/core.html#loglevel. The author has altered or added some text.

Log level	Description	Example
alert	Action must be taken immediately. These are errors that should be fixed as soon as possible, but won't interfere with Apache's startup or shutdown. For example, if the server cannot determine its own domain name and switches over to its IP address.	"getpwuid: couldn't determine username from uid"
crit	Critical conditions. Errors marked critical indicate problems with Apache's normal operation. The example at right shows that Apache attempted to open a socket (a connection through which data is sent), and failed. These errors should be fixed relatively quickly when spotted.	"socket: failed to get a socket, exiting child."
error	Error conditions, indicating standard errors in operation, are still important. For example, if you haven't configured the DocumentRoot, an error condition will appear, informing you that the directory doesn't exist. Often, CGI scripts can cause entries in the error.log, such as the one in the example at right.	"Premature end of script headers"
warn	Warning conditions. These aren't necessarily errors, and usually indicate problems that Apache was able to recover from.	"child process 1234 did not exit, sending another SIGHUP"
notice	Normal but significant condition. These tend to be operational messages, such as Apache being started or stopped.	"httpd:caught SIGBUS, attempting to drop core in..."
info	Informational. Doesn't necessarily indicate an actual error. In the following example, Apache has noticed an increase in traffic beyond what it can handle, and it has logged the problem along with a solution.	"Server seems busy, (you may need to increase StartServers, or Min/MaxSpareServers)"
debug	Debug-level messages. This means everything.	"Opening config file..."

The further down the list you go for your LogLevel setting, the more verbose your error log will become. For example, a LogLevel of Debug will be filled with much more information than a LogLevel of Crit. The Apache documentation recommends a LogLevel of warn, and I'd agree with them.

It's likely that you'll never look at error.log unless things start going wrong, so you should try and keep the file as small as possible. By selecting warn as your LogLevel, you'll be able to catch problems that may be slowing your web server down or causing it to not work at all.

The format of the LogLevel entry will look like this:

```
LogLevel warn
```

access.log

The access.log file contains a record of every single request sent to your Apache web server. For a single web page, several entries are often entered into the access.log, one for the web page itself, followed by one for each of the web page's support files (images, external Cascading Style Sheet (CSS) files, and so on). It'll take some time, but eventually you'll have no problems following a thread through the log file.

Formatting the access log

The LogFormat and CustomLog directives are used to format and create Apache log files. LogFormat sets up the contents of the log file. Multiple LogFormat entries are allowed, but must have unique aliases.

Combined logs

The following is the syntax of the CustomLog directive:

```
LogFormat "<options>" <alias>
```

A sample CustomLog can be found in the default httpd.conf, as follows:

```
LogFormat "%h %l %u %t \"%r\" %>s %b \"%{Referer}i\" \"%{User-
Agent}i\"" combined
```

> *Double quotes must be escaped inside the LogFormat options. To escape the double quotes, use a backslash (for example, \ ").*

Any text entered within the LogFormat directive's options will appear in the log file. A full list of options can be seen in the following table.[2]

---

[2] See the "Apache HTTP Server Version 1.3" page at http://httpd.apache.org/docs/mod/ mod_log_config.html. The author has altered or added some text.

The default httpd.conf includes several preconfigured LogFormat aliases, including full, debug, combined, common, referrer, and agent. Most of the time, this is going to be more than enough for you.

Variable	Reports	Should you include it?
%a	The IP address making the HTTP request.	Yes. It's included in all the default log formats.
%A	Local IP address.	Not really. You already know your IP address, and it's not that helpful when creating statistics of your site. However, if you are running multiple servers and combining the logs, this may be useful to tell you which server the log entry is referring to.
%B	Bytes sent to the browser, not including HTTP headers.	No. Although this is useful information, it is not in Common Log Format (CLF). Instead, use %b.
%b	Bytes sent to the browser, not including HTTP headers. This attribute records the data in CLF format, however, recording a hyphen (-) instead of a 0 when no data is sent.	Yes. Having the amount of data transferred is extremely important in generating site-traffic statistics. Recording this data in CLF format ensures that any statistics package you use will understand the information.
%c	Connection status when response was completed. The following are recorded: X: The connection was aborted before the response was completed. +: Connection may be kept alive after the response is sent. -: The connection will be closed after the response is sent.	No. This information is really only useful for debugging problems with the web server.
%{VAR}e	Contents of the environment variable VAR.	No. Only use this if you need to store the contents of session variables to a log file outside of a scripted environment.
%f	File name requested.	No. This is included in the %r option.
%h	Remote host.	Yes.

(Continued)

Variable	Reports	Should you include it?
%H	Request protocol.	No. This is included in the %r option.
%{VAR}i	Displays the content of the specified header variable. Replace VAR with the header variable you want to display. For more information about header variables, consult www.w3.org/Protocols/HTTP/ Object_Headers.html. %{Referer}i is included in the default httpd.conf.	Yes, for specific information, such as referrers.
%l	The remote log name.	Yes, but only because it is included by default.
%m	The request method used by the browser.	No. This is included in the %r option.
%{VAR}n	The contents of a note from the specified module. Replace VAR with the name of the note.	No.
%{VAR}o	The contents of a specific header line in the server's reply. Replace VAR with the name of the header.	No. Only include this if you need to find out specific information for debugging or troubleshooting.
%p	The port the web server is running on.	No. Only use this if you are combining logs from servers running on different ports.
%P	The process ID of the Apache session that serviced the request.	No. This should only be used for troubleshooting purposes.
%q	The query string passed along with the URL. If no query string is passed, this will return no values.	No. This will be included with the %r option.
%r	The first line of the incoming HTTP request. This includes the HTTP version, the request method, and the URL requested.	Yes. This is one of the more useful logging options.

8

(Continued)

Variable	Reports	Should you include it?
%s	The status of the original request.	No. This will report the first request made, including forwarded pages. Use %>s instead.
%>s	The status of the last request.	Yes.
%t	The time in CLF that the request was made. The CLF time format looks like this: [07/Dec/2003:13:15:32 -0700].	Yes.
%{format}t	Use this option to change the time format. The available time formats are viewable at http://unixhelp.ed.ac.uk/ CGI/man-cgi?strftime+3.	No. Only change this if you require a standard time format that is different from the one supplied by the %t option.
%T	The time taken to serve the request, in seconds.	No. This is only useful for server and script benchmarks.
%u	Remote user name. This is the name of the person logged in to your web server via htaccess.	Yes, but only because it's included by default. This option is also useful if you are using htaccess to restrict access to directories on your web server.
%U	The URL requested, not including the query string. For example, if the requested URL was /scripts/search.php? keyword=foobar, the value returned by the %U option would be /scripts/search.php.	No. This is covered by the %r option.
%v	The server name of the Apache server.	No. Only use this if you are combining log files and need to know the name of the server.
%V	The server name of the Apache server, according to the UseCanonicalName setting.	No. Only use this if you are combining log files and need to know the name of the server.

The CustomLog directive tells Apache where to place the file, and what LogFormat to use. The CustomLog directive uses the following syntax:

```
CustomLog /path/to/logfile alias
```

An example of this would be the following:

```
CustomLog /var/log/apache/access.log combined
```

This would write a log entry to the file /var/log/apache/access.log using the combined LogFormat mentioned earlier. You can create multiple CustomLog entries, but each one must point to a unique file in order to avoid conflicts.

As you can see, the default CustomLog and LogFormat directives are pretty useful. However, you may want to change the format of the log entry to better suit your purposes. For example, you may want to change the LogFormat to include a comma as a delimiter between the parts of a log file for easier importing into Excel. Or, you may want to change the order of elements within the entry, or add information not included by default. To do so, use the previous table of options to create your own CustomLog file directives in httpd.conf.

> *Changing the default LogFormat string can have undesirable effects, especially if you're using software to analyze and create statistics on your website. Only change this if you're really, really certain that you want to and you know what effects it will have.*

Multiple log files

If you're not a big fan of monolithic log files, you can break them up into several smaller files, each of which can contain specific information. The process is identical to setting up the combined log file, but instead of containing a full suite of information, only specific information is written down. For example, you could have different logs for referrers, agents (browsers), and users. This would take the following form in your httpd.conf configuration file:

```
LogFormat "%h %t \"%r\" %>s %b \"%{Referer}i\" " referrer
LogFormat "%h %t \"%r\" %>s %b \"%{User-Agent}i\" " agent
LogFormat "%h %t \"%r\" %>s %b %u" user
CustomLog referrers.log referrer
CustomLog agents.log agent
CustomLog users.log user
```

Using the parameters from the previous table with multiple logs, you can capture almost every conceivable piece of information about your website in an easy-to-access format.

Conditional log files

Apache also gives you the ability to conditionally log information. For example, you may want to log your computer's access to the Apache server in a different log file than other users of the server. To do so, you'll need to make use of the SetEnvIf directive.

The SetEnvIf directive lets you create environment variables for use by other directives if a condition is met. In this case, you're going to use the SetEnv directive to create an environment variable called nolog if the remote address accessing the website is your IP

8

(let's say your IP is 192.168.1.103), then you'll write to the log file if the nolog variable isn't set. Your httpd.conf entry would look something like this:

```
SetEnvIf Remote_Addr "192.168.1.103" nolog
CustomLog access.log combined !nolog
```

Reading the log

My partner recently went on a research trip for her dissertation and had to learn how to read sixteenth-century handwriting. It occurred to me, as I sat there watching her, that reading through an Apache log file entry isn't all that different. Both the sixteenth-century handscript and the Apache log file entry look like an unrecognizable mess. However, when you break it down into recognizable parts, it becomes much easier to understand. Each entry in the access.log contains a wealth of information—it's just a matter of learning how to read it.

The following is a fairly typical entry in the access.log:

```
65.110.12.164 - darren  [04/Oct/2003:16:52:19 -0700] "GET
 /scripts/search.php?searchterm=images HTTP/1.1" 200
41418 "http://staticred.net/scripts/search.php"
Mozilla/4.0 (compatible; MSIE 6.0; Windows NT
5.0)"
```

Log entry	What it means
65.110.12.164	This is the IP the request originated from. The previous request originated from the IP address 65.110.12.164. Often this field will contain a hostname instead of an IP address—for example, staticred.net or dialh2434.someprovider.net. Knowing the IP address or hostname is extremely important for tracking user visits, paths taken through the site, and so on.
-	This is a spot reserved for the Apache server's IP address. This is not recorded by default.
darren	This is the authenticated user who requested the page. This should only be recorded if a user has authenticated herself through Apache before requesting the page. Once she has authenticated on the Apache server, however, her username will be recorded with every request that she makes. Refer back to the section in Chapter 3 where I discussed the .htaccess and .htpasswd files, for more information on this. In this case, the user "darren" requested the page. Hey, that name looks familiar.

(Continued)

Log entry	What it means
[04/Oct/2003:16:52:19 -0700]	This is the date the request was made, recorded down to the second. This entry also includes the timezone the server exists in.
"GET /scripts/search.php?searchterm=images HTTP/1.1"	This is the request method, URL, and HTTP version sent to Apache from the browser. In this case, a GET request was made for search.php in the /scripts directory with a command-line argument of searchterm=images, by a browser using version 1.1 of the HTTP protocol.
	Apache reads this request as a user sending information to the file /scripts/search.php. The browser agent has told the server that it knows the 1.1 version of the HTTP protocol, so all communications will be sent using that version of the HTTP protocol. Since there are minor differences between versions of the HTTP protocol, it's important for Apache to know this. Note: The path referred to in this part of the log-file entry isn't the physical path of the file on the server. It's the relative path to the DocumentRoot directory that's set up in your httpd.conf file for the domain. For example, if your DocumentRoot was configured to be /var/www, the file accessed would actually exist at /var/www/scripts/search.php. It seems like a minor point, but I've known a few people who are confused by this.
200	This is the HTTP code sent to the browser. In this case, the file requested exists on the server, so a code 200 (OK) is sent to the browser. If the file didn't exist, a 404 error message would be recorded.
41418	The number of bytes transferred to the browser is also recorded for statistics. In this case, the script sent 41,418 bytes of information. This part of the log entry can be very useful for troubleshooting scripts, or for calculating the amount of data transferred for a given period or file.

8

(Continued)

Log entry	What it means
"http://staticred.net/scripts/ search.php"	This field shows the referrer, or page that directed the client to this request. In this example, you can see that the user loaded the search.php file, and is now viewing the results of their search term ("images"). If there was no referrer (otherwise known as a direct request), this field will simply show a hyphen. Direct requests are often common for graphic files, Flash files, or any other file type included in a web page.
"Mozilla/4.0 (compatible; MSIE 6.0; Windows NT 5.0)"	The user agent (the user's browser and version) is the final piece of the log-entry puzzle. In the previous example, the user is viewing the site in Internet Explorer 6.0 on Windows 2000. Obtaining the user agent is really very helpful when auditing the site design and code. If you know that 95 percent of your users are viewing the site with newer browsers, you can take advantage of technologies supported by those browsers. Likewise, if 25 percent of your users are still using older browsers that don't support the newer technologies, you know ahead of time that you should rethink using them. This part of the log entry gets a bit sticky, since it's one of the few pieces of information sent directly from the browser. Some browser manufacturers don't identify themselves, or identify themselves as another browser. For example, the Opera browser can be configured to identify itself as Opera, Mozilla, or a number of versions of Internet Explorer. Likewise, search engines often identify themselves as other browsers as well. If you need to take completely accurate browser metrics, you might want to consider using a JavaScript or Document Object Model (DOM) solution. If you only need to get metrics on the major browsers, then entries in the log files will be more than adequate. Regardless, the information in this part of the entry is important if you're using server-level browser detection (for example, a PHP or Perl file), since this is the information that will be passed along to your script by the server.

Where can I find Apache's log files?

The location of Apache's log files is configurable within the httpd.conf file, and can vary if you're running multiple sites on a single Apache server. Generally, however, you can find the files in the default log directory. On a Linux system, they can be found in the /var/log/apache directory. On a Windows system, they can be found in your Apache program folder, in the logs subfolder.

Configuring Apache logs

By default, Apache's logging is pretty good; it keeps a basic level of information about the Apache executable in the error.log, and tracks most client information in the access.log. It's likely that you won't have to change the default settings for logging. That is, until something starts going wrong. So I'll save you a throbbing headache and show you how to configure logging to capture problems before they become unsolvable.

This table details the directives used when configuring Apache log files.

Directive	Function
HostNameLookups	Configures Apache to look up the hostname for a given IP address and then record it in the log files.
ErrorLog	Configures the name and the location of Apache's error log. This log will record all activities of the Apache application, depending on which LogLevel is set.
LogLevel	Configures the detail to include in the Apache error log.
LogFormat	Configures which information will be included in Apache's access logs. Multiple LogFormats can be configured, each with their own unique alias.
CustomLog	Configures the file location and LogFormat to use. Multiple CustomLog entries can be configured.

8

Log files for virtual hosts

If you're running multiple domains from a single Apache web server, it's a good idea to create separate logs for each domain. Although you certainly can place everything into a single log file, it's generally not a good idea. With the standard access.log LogFormat, there will be no identifying marks to determine which domains were accessed in any given entry.

A good convention to follow is to use the prefix of the file names of each log with the domain name. For example, the log files for staticred.net are named staticred_access.log and staticred_error.log. In this way, you can easily access log files for a specific name without having to search through a monolithic log file.

split-logfile

If you don't want to create separate log files for each virtual host, you can make use of a small Perl script included with Apache, called split-logfile. This script takes a supplied log file, and breaks it into separate files based on the first part of each log entry.

Before starting, you will want to add %v to the start of your CustomLog directive. This starts the log file with the virtual host's domain name. The split-logfile script will see this and create a file for each virtual host contained within the access.log. You'll also want to create a world-readable directory for the split log files to be created in. This will allow you to keep your original access.log file (and the directory it resides in) untouched.

The script's usage is pretty simple:

```
perl split-logfile < access.log
```

Another script, logcron, is available for Linux and Mac OS X servers at http://slacksite.com/apache/scripts/logcron. This script copies your access log to another location, then creates the split log files using the split-logfile script. The script is well commented, so you'll be able to configure it easily.

For more information on virtual hosts, refer to Chapter 4.

Rotating log files

If a website is popular, Apache's log files can grow to an unwieldy size fairly rapidly. Since Apache records every access to the website, it's likely that it will record tens of thousands of lines of data every day. The more popular a site is, and the more supporting files it uses in its design, the more lines Apache will write to the log files.

A strategy to handle the problem of file size is to enable rotating log files in Apache. Rotating the log files allows you to maintain several smaller log files, which automatically archive themselves. Beyond the first archive, the files are often archived to save space.

The archived files keep the same file name, but have a number appended to them that grows with their age. For example, if you had ten archive files, the newest archive file would be access.log.0, while the oldest would be access.log.9.gz.

I would recommend keeping about a year's worth of log files at any given time. Log files after that point aren't going to be very useful for gathering information about your website beyond comparison purposes. If you really want to keep all of your web logs, simply back them up to an alternate location once every month or so.

How to configure log rotation

Older versions of Apache used to configure log rotation within the httpd.conf file. However, recent versions use a third-party application, called logrotate. This is installed by default on most Linux distributions using Apache, and makes the rotation of logs quite simple. logrotate is configured through the file /etc/logrotate.d/apache.

A sample logrotate configuration file for Apache looks like this:

```
/var/log/apache/*.log {
        weekly
        missingok
        rotate 52
        compress
        delaycompress
        notifempty
        create 640 root adm
        sharedscripts
        postrotate
                /etc/init.d/apache reload > /dev/null
        endscript
}
```

Let's break this down. The first line tells logrotate where to find the log files. In this case, it's being told to look in /var/log/apache for all files with a .log extension. It then opens the options directives with an open curly bracket ({).

```
/var/log/apache/*.log {
```

The next lines indicate which options to set for logrotate. These options are outlined in the following table.[3]

Option	Description
compress	Old versions of log files are compressed with gzip by default. See also nocompress.
compresscmd	Specifies which command to use to compress log files. The default is gzip. See also compress.
uncompresscmd	Specifies which command to use to uncompress log files. The default is gunzip.
compressext	Specifies which extension to use on compressed log files, if compression is enabled. The default follows that of the configured compression command.

(Continued)

[3] See "logrotate (8)—Linux main page" at www.die.net/doc/linux/man/man8/logrotate.8.html. The author has altered or added some text.

Option	Description
compressoptions	Command-line options may be passed to the compression program, if one is in use. The default for gzip is "-9" (maximum compression).
copy	Make a copy of the log file, but don't change the original at all. This option can be used, for instance, to make a snapshot of the current log file, or when some other utility needs to truncate or parse the file. When this option is used, the create option will have no effect, as the old log file stays in place.
copytruncate	Truncate the original log file in place after creating a copy, instead of moving the old log file and optionally creating a new one. It can be used when some program cannot be told to close its log file and thus might continue writing (appending) to the previous log file forever. Note that there is a very small time slice between copying the file and truncating it, so some logging data might be lost. When this option is used, the create option will have no effect, as the old log file stays in place.
create mode owner group	Immediately after rotation (before the postrotate script is run) the log file is created (with the same name as the log file just rotated). mode specifies the mode for the log file in octal (the same as chmod(2)); owner specifies the username that will own the log file; and group specifies the group the log file will belong to. Any of the log-file attributes may be omitted, in which case those attributes for the new file will use the same values as the original log file for the omitted attributes. This option can be disabled using the nocreate option.
daily	Log files are rotated every day.
delaycompress	Postpone compression of the previous log file to the next rotation cycle. This only has an effect when used in combination with compress. It can be used when some program cannot be told to close its log file and thus might continue writing to the previous log file for some time.
extension ext	Log files are given the final extension .ext after rotation. If compression is used, the compression extension (normally .gz) appears after ext.
ifempty	Rotate the log file even if it's empty, overriding the notifempty option (ifempty is the default).

(Continued)

Option	Description
include file_or_directory	Reads the file given as an argument as if it was included inline where the include directive appears. If a directory is given, most of the files in that directory are read in alphabetical order before processing of the including file continues. The only files that are ignored are files that aren't regular files (such as directories and named pipes) and files whose names end with one of the taboo extensions, as specified by the tabooext directive. The include directive may not appear inside of a log-file definition.
mail address	When a log is rotated out of existence, it's mailed to address. If no mail should be generated by a particular log, the nomail directive may be used.
mailfirst	When using the mail command, mail the just-rotated file instead of the about-to-expire file.
maillast	When using the mail command, mail the about-to-expire file instead of the just-rotated file (this is the default).
missingok	If the log file is missing, go on to the next one without issuing an error message. See also nomissingok.
monthly	Log files are rotated the first time logrotate is run in a month (this is normally on the first day of the month).
nocompress	Old versions of log files aren't compressed with gzip. See also compress.
nocopy	Don't copy the original log file and leave it in place (this overrides the copy option).
nocopytruncate	Don't truncate the original log file in place after creating a copy (this overrides the copytruncate option).
nocreate	New log files are not created (this overrides the create option).
nodelaycompress	Don't postpone compression of the previous log file to the next rotation cycle (this overrides the delaycompress option).
nomail	Don't mail old log files to any address.
nomissingok	If a log file does not exist, issue an error. This is the default.

(Continued)

8

Option	Description
noolddir	Logs are rotated in the same directory the log normally resides in (this overrides the olddir option).
nosharedscripts	Run prerotate and postrotate scripts for every script that is rotated (this is the default, and overrides the sharedscripts option).
notifempty	Don't rotate the log if it is empty (this overrides the ifempty option).
olddir directory	Logs are moved into directory for rotation. The directory must be on the same physical device as the log file being rotated. When this option is used all old versions of the log end up in directory. This option may be overridden by the noolddir option.
postrotate/endscript	The lines between postrotate and endscript (both of which must appear on lines by themselves) are executed after the log file is rotated. These directives may only appear inside of a log file definition. See prerotate as well.
prerotate/endscript	The lines between prerotate and endscript (both of which must appear on lines by themselves) are executed before the log file is rotated and only if the log will actually be rotated. These directives may only appear inside of a log file definition. See postrotate as well.
rotate count	Log files are rotated count times before being removed or mailed to the address specified in a mail directive. If count is 0, old versions are removed rather then rotated.
size size	Log files are rotated when they grow bigger then size bytes. If size is followed by M, the size if assumed to be in megabytes. If k is used, the size is in kilobytes. So size 100, size 100k, and size 100M are all valid.
sharedscripts	Normally, prescript and postscript scripts are run for each log which is rotated, meaning that a single script may be run multiple times for log file entries that match multiple files (such as the /var/log/news/* example). If sharedscripts is specified, the scripts are only run once, no matter how many logs match the wildcarded pattern. However, if none of the logs in the pattern require rotating, the scripts will not be run at all. This option overrides the nosharedscripts option.

(Continued)

Option	Description
start count	This is the number to use as the base for rotation. For example, if you specify 0, the logs will be created with a .0 extension as they are rotated from the original log files. If you specify 9, log files will be created with a .9, skipping 0–8. Files will still be rotated the number of times specified with the count directive.
tabooext [+] list	The current taboo extension list is changed (see the include directive for information on the taboo extensions). If a + precedes the list of extensions, the current taboo extension list is augmented; otherwise it is replaced. At startup, the taboo extension list contains .rpmorig, .rpmsave, ,v, .swp, .rpmnew, and ~.
weekly	Log files are rotated if the current weekday is less then the weekday of the last rotation or if more than a week has passed since the last rotation. This is normally the same as rotating logs on the first day of the week, but it works better if logrotate is not run every night.

Piped logs

If you're a Windows user, or if you don't have access to logrotate, you can use piped logs. If you configure Apache to use piped logs it runs an external program (a process called piping) any time the log files are written to.

To configure piped logs, simply start the TransferLog directive's options with a pipe (|). This will signal to Apache that it needs to launch the application. One such external program is rotatelogs, which is included with the Apache binaries. The rotatelogs utility is a more basic form of logrotate that doesn't support compression.

The rotatelogs utility takes one of two command-line arguments: a time in seconds or a file size. These command-line arguments tell rotatelogs when it should close one log file, archive it, and start another. An example entry in httpd.conf for rotatelogs would look like this:

```
TransferLog "|rotatelogs /path/to/logs/access.log 86400"
```

This would pass the contents of the access.log file once every 24 hours. To tell rotatelogs to rotate the log after reaching 5 MB in size, you would use the following entry:

```
TransferLog "|rotatelogs /path/to/logs/access.log 5M"
```

Reading archived log files

In order to save space, archived log files are often compressed using the gzip compression scheme. In order to read them, you have to either uncompress their contents or use a text editor that supports reading gzipped files.

8

Under Linux, you can read gzipped text files using the vi editor, which is installed by default on most systems. You can search through them using the zgrep command, which is identical to the grep command. Check out the appendix for links to useful information on both of these Linux applications. Otherwise, you'll have to uncompress the files.

Under Windows, you'll have to uncompress the archived files to a temporary directory using a program such as WinZip, then view them with a text editor.

What do I do with all these access logs?

Apache's log files are a very useful resource for creating statistics on your website. Because the access.log records every piece of available information, log files can be used to determine your site's usage, its traffic patterns, where your visitors are coming from, or its missing pages.

As you've already seen, unless you've been a bad reader and skipped ahead, the access.log records pretty much anything and everything you'll ever want to know. You have access to pages requested, files sent, kilobytes transferred, browsers used, and much, much more. It's marketing gold: Not only can you see what your clients are looking at, but how they got there, what browser they used to view it, how long they spent browsing other pages, and in some cases even the geographical region they were browsing from.

By aggregating and analyzing all this data, you can better direct the content development of your website, create marketing plans that effectively target members of your audience, and make use of technologies that are supported by the browsers your clients use. It's all a question of how to aggregate and analyze the data.

Using log-analysis programs

The raw log files are strongly beneficial to have, but they're a nightmare when it comes to actually doing anything useful with them. A standard entry, as you've already seen, contains a large amount of information; now, consider the entries for support files and multiply that by hundreds or thousands of entries a day. It quickly becomes an untamed beast, and unless you're some kind of mathematical god who is able to remember and process massive amounts of information, trying to make any sense of all that information is going to become impossible very quickly.

As a result, several programmers have come up with applications that analyze your log files and create statistics for the information kept within them. There are literally hundreds of them, but I'll break it down to three of the most common: Analog, Webalizer, and WebTrends. Analog and Webalizer are both available free of charge, and can be used by any person or organization. WebTrends is a commercial application and can be bought as a hosted service or an application.

Historically, people have left their statistics pages in unprotected directories on their website. I did this for quite some time on both my personal domain and the academic journal I run. However, this type of marketing information is becoming more and more valuable.

It now makes complete sense to protect this data as much as you would any other data in your organization. If you have an intranet server, consider hosting the statistics site there. Otherwise, make sure that you password-protect the output directory of your statistics.

Analog

Analog (www.analog.cx) is one of the most established log-analysis packages available, and has been around almost as long as Apache has. Analog's statistics are fairly basic, and include the following:

- Monthly, daily and hourly summaries of site traffic
- Operating systems
- Status code reports
- User agents
- Referrers
- Search word reports
- File-type reports
- File-size reports
- Geographical information

Analog isn't going to win any design awards, but it will get you the basic information in a quick and easy-to-use fashion. Plus, it's free, which wins it all sorts of support. A standard installation looks something like this:

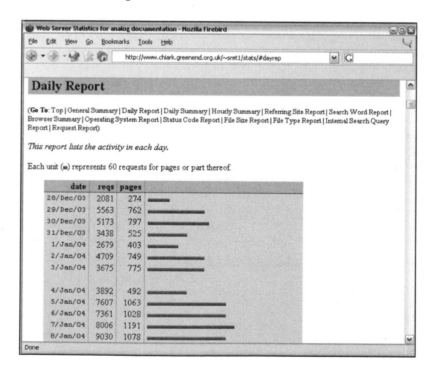

Analog runs as a scheduled task under your operating system, at whatever interval you specify. Log files can grow relatively quickly; as a result, it takes a fair amount of time to run through them all. Though there are web applications out there that will do a live analysis of your log files, they will generally only analyze a small portion or will be very slow to calculate. By analyzing the files at a predetermined time, you get relatively up-to-date statistics that are at your fingertips immediately. A half-hour's worth of data isn't going to make too much of a difference when you're trending statistics over the period of a month.

Both Windows and Linux offer methods to create scheduled tasks. Windows 2000 and XP use the Task Scheduler to run applications on a scheduled basis and Linux uses cron. Of the two, Windows is the easier to use—simply open the Task Scheduler, drag and drop the Analog program file into it, then set your schedule. Life couldn't be easier.

I wish it were that easy for Linux. Although cron is somewhat more powerful than Task Scheduler, it's also more complicated; Like Apache, cron uses a text file for its configuration, called .crontab. However, you can't edit the crontab in a normal text editor. To edit the crontab, you have to run the command crontab -e, then enter a new line for your application. A sample crontab line would look like this:

```
01 * * * * analog -q > /dev/null  2>&1
```

This would run Analog on the first minute of every hour, using a specific configuration file. The nonsense at the end is for the benefit of you and your user logs: It suppresses any output, including its launch being recorded in the system logs.

Webalizer

Webalizer (www.mrunix.net/webalizer/) is a bit of a step up from Analog. Though it still offers basic information about the site, it offers it in a very user-friendly, configurable way. Webalizer also packages its output into a more attractive presentation by default, and separates the information in a very logical way. I prefer using Webalizer for my own sites, because it offers me a little more flexibility in presentation. A standard installation of Webalizer is shown on the following page.

Webalizer also separates the content of the statistics from its presentation; header and footer files can be configured to fit the output into an existing site template.

Webalizer shows you the following information:

- File statistics, such as bytes and number of files transferred
- Number of hits, visits, and unique sites broken down by month and day
- User agents
- Referrers
- Geographical information
- Referrers

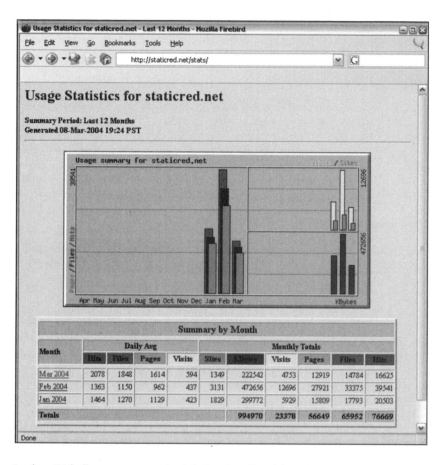

Like Analog, Webalizer runs as a scheduled task under either Linux or Windows; as a result, you can have your statistics as up to date as you'd like. Given that running Webalizer takes system resources away from your web server, I recommend updating the statistics once an hour or so, depending on how important the information is to you.

Webalizer has two components: the directory containing the executable and configuration files and the output directory. As you've probably guessed by now, the output directory contains the HTML versions of Webalizer's reports. It also contains the history files Webalizer relies on to generate them. The program directory contains the actual executable files and configuration files, which Webalizer depends on to run.

Webalizer's output directory can be installed anywhere that's web accessible, as there are no script elements to the package. I would, however, recommend that you keep the Webalizer executable and configuration files in a non-web-accessible location. You can run Webalizer on a separate machine from your Apache server, as long as it has direct access to the Apache log files.

I would recommend backing up your Webalizer output directory, as it contains Webalizer's history files. Without these history files, Webalizer will not be able to generate the historical statistics.

WebTrends

WebTrends (www.webtrends.com) has become extremely popular among Windows users and Windows-focused managers. Like Webalizer, WebTrends is an executable file run that generates statistics. Unlike Webalizer, WebTrends also outputs its reports to Word and Excel, for easy statistics generation, and offers the ability to track routes taken through the website, track marketing programs, and more.

WebTrends also supports log files from many different web servers, such as Internet Information Server (IIS), Lotus Domino, NetWare, and others. If you're running a hybrid network with many different web servers, then this is a definite plus.

Of course, none of this comes for free: it can cost up to $10,500 for the Enterprise software, or $1000 per month for their hosted service. If you have a spare $11,000 handy, then definitely get a license for the software. You'll have better, more comprehensive statistics than any other web-statistics package out there. However, if you're like the rest of us poor slobs, Analog or Webalizer will more than cover your basic needs and you (or your friendly neighborhood Perl hacker) can write scripts to accomplish the rest. To see how the other side lives, you can download a 14-day trial version of the Webalizer software, and then use it to determine what statistics you find helpful, so you can write scripts to accomplish them.

Creating custom scripts

Sometimes, a log-analysis package won't always fit your needs. I discovered this a few months ago, when I needed the ability to search my log files for a specific term. I already knew enough PHP to get myself into trouble, so I decided that it would be faster and more efficient if I wrote a script to do it for me, instead of searching through Google results.

One of the benefits of the script I wrote was that I could use the same search functionality to track users' paths through the site—I simply had to search the logs for their hostname. The script I used can be found on the friends of ED website (www.friendsofed.com), or you can try it at http://staticred.net/scripts/search.php.

Troubleshooting with Apache

As I mentioned at the start of this chapter, you can also use the Apache logs to troubleshoot problems with scripts and Apache itself.

Tracking down 404 errors and learning why they occur

Perhaps one of the most useful troubleshooting capabilities of Apache's log files is tracking down 404 errors (missing files) on your website, and finding where they were referred from. In the "Reading the log" section, I discussed the structure of a log-file entry for a successful page view. The structure for the log file is nearly identical for missing files. The only difference is that a 404 is recorded instead of a 200 for the HTTP result code.

Because the entry in the access.log is recorded identically for a missing file as it is for an existing file, all the information about the request is available, including a referrer (can you see where I'm going with this?). As a result, you can see where the page request originated. If the page request originated on your server, you know exactly where to go to fix the problem.

In fact, because you know the result code for a missing file, you could even write a script to search for missing files in your Apache logs and report which requests are spawning 404 errors, and finally, where they're coming from.

Summing it up

Now that you've had a good overview about how logs work in Apache, and how to configure them, you're just about ready to become an Apache superstar. You not only can configure custom logs for your websites, but you can ensure that virtual hosts running on your Apache server have their own host-specific log files.

8

In the next chapter, you're going to build on all the knowledge you've gained so far, and you'll see some sample Apache configurations.

9 SAMPLE APACHE CONFIGURATIONS

This chapter sets up several scenarios and shows you how to best configure Apache to handle each one. For all of the following scenarios, I'm going to create some configuration template files, which will be included in the httpd.conf configuration file. These template files are as follows:

- basic.conf, which will contain the basic configuration options
- modules.conf, which will contain the base set of modules
- logfiles.conf, which will contain the standard log file configuration

You don't have to make these files yourself—I've done this here in order to avoid repeating the same directives over and over again. If you're going to use the following samples, make sure you create these files and place them in your Apache configuration directory. I've included the contents here. Windows users: don't forget to replace the UNIX directory references with the path to your Apache program directory. In the following samples, these files are included using the Include directive.

Several common scenarios follow; since I've already covered the directives used in these sample configurations, I won't go into too much detail here. I'll let you know what chapters to go back and review in each sample. In each sample configuration I've bolded the sections that are unique to the scenario.

The basic.conf file will contain all the global directives, such as ServerRoot, DocumentRoot, and Port. These directives won't change between the different sample configurations.

> *Windows users will have to replace the paths specified for ServerRoot, LockFile, and PidFile directives with paths to the files within your Apache program folder. The following are examples of how the LockFile, PidFile, and ServerRoot directives might be configured:*
>
> *LockFile logs\apache.lock*
>
> *PidFile logs\apache.pid*
>
> *ServerRoot C:\htdocs*
>
> *The ScoreBoardFile directive isn't used under Windows.*

```
ServerType standalone
ServerRoot /etc/apache
LockFile /var/lock/apache.lock
PidFile /var/run/apache.pid
ScoreBoardFile /var/run/apache.scoreboard
Timeout 300
Keepalive on
MaxKeepAliveRequests 100
```

```
KeepAliveTimeout 15
MinSpareServers 5
MaxSpareServers 10
StartServers 5
Max Clients 150
MaxRequestsPerChild 100
ExtendedStatus on
Port 80
User www-data
Group www-data
ServerSignature on
AccessFileName .htaccess
DefaultType text/plain
HostNameLookups off
# prevent direct access of .htaccess and .htpasswd files.
<Files ~ "^\.ht">
    Order allow,deny
    Deny from all
</Files>
UseCanonicalName On
TypesConfig /etc/mime.types
<IfModule mod_dir.c>
    DirectoryIndex index.html index.php index.htm index.shtml index.cgi
</IfModule>
```

The modules.conf configuration file contains all modules you're likely to need in the following configurations. Modules not included in this file will be included in these samples.

> *Many of the modules in this list are left commented—it's a good idea to keep them in, just in case you have to load them in the future.*

```
# LoadModule vhost_alias_module /usr/lib/apache/1.3/mod_vhost_alias.so
# LoadModule env_module /usr/lib/apache/1.3/mod_env.so
LoadModule config_log_module /usr/lib/apache/1.3/mod_log_config.so
LoadModule mime_magic_module /usr/lib/apache/1.3/mod_mime_magic.so
LoadModule mime_module /usr/lib/apache/1.3/mod_mime.so
LoadModule negotiation_module /usr/lib/apache/1.3/mod_negotiation.so
LoadModule status_module /usr/lib/apache/1.3/mod_status.so
# LoadModule info_module /usr/lib/apache/1.3/mod_info.so
# LoadModule includes_module /usr/lib/apache/1.3/mod_include.so
LoadModule autoindex_module /usr/lib/apache/1.3/mod_autoindex.so
LoadModule dir_module /usr/lib/apache/1.3/mod_dir.so
LoadModule cgi_module /usr/lib/apache/1.3/mod_cgi.so
# LoadModule asis_module /usr/lib/apache/1.3/mod_asis.so
```

```
# LoadModule imap_module /usr/lib/apache/1.3/mod_imap.so
# LoadModule action_module /usr/lib/apache/1.3/mod_actions.so
# LoadModule speling_module /usr/lib/apache/1.3/mod_speling.so
# LoadModule userdir_module /usr/lib/apache/1.3/mod_userdir.so
LoadModule alias_module /usr/lib/apache/1.3/mod_alias.so
LoadModule rewrite_module /usr/lib/apache/1.3/mod_rewrite.so
LoadModule access_module /usr/lib/apache/1.3/mod_access.so
LoadModule auth_module /usr/lib/apache/1.3/mod_auth.so
# LoadModule anon_auth_module /usr/lib/apache/1.3/mod_auth_anon.so
# LoadModule dbm_auth_module /usr/lib/apache/1.3/mod_auth_dbm.so
# LoadModule db_auth_module /usr/lib/apache/1.3/mod_auth_db.so
# LoadModule proxy_module /usr/lib/apache/1.3/libproxy.so
 LoadModule digest_module /usr/lib/apache/1.3/mod_digest.so
# LoadModule cern_meta_module /usr/lib/apache/1.3/mod_cern_meta.so
LoadModule expires_module /usr/lib/apache/1.3/mod_expires.so
# LoadModule headers_module /usr/lib/apache/1.3/mod_headers.so
# LoadModule usertrack_module /usr/lib/apache/1.3/mod_usertrack.so
LoadModule unique_id_module /usr/lib/apache/1.3/mod_unique_id.so
LoadModule setenvif_module /usr/lib/apache/1.3/mod_setenvif.so
# LoadModule sys_auth_module /usr/lib/apache/1.3/mod_auth_sys.so
# LoadModule put_module /usr/lib/apache/1.3/mod_put.so
# LoadModule throttle_module /usr/lib/apache/1.3/mod_throttle.so
# LoadModule allowdev_module /usr/lib/apache/1.3/mod_allowdev.so
# LoadModule eaccess_module /usr/lib/apache/1.3/mod_eaccess.so
# LoadModule php4_module /usr/lib/apache/1.3/libphp4.so
# LoadModule roaming_module /usr/lib/apache/1.3/mod_roaming.so
```

Finally, the logfiles.conf configuration file contains the configuration for the Apache server's log files, as follows:

```
LogLevel warn
LogFormat "%h %l %u %t \"%r\"%c %>s %b \"%{Referer}i\" \"%
➡{User-Agent}i\" %T %v" full
LogFormat "%h %l %u %t \"%r\" %>s %b \"%{Referer}i\" \"%
➡{User-Agent}i\" %P %T" debug
LogFormat "%h %l %u %t \"%r\" %>s %b \"%{Referer}i\" \"%
➡{User-Agent}i\"" combined
LogFormat "%h %l %u %t \"%r\" %>s %b" common
LogFormat "%{Referer}i -> %U" referer
LogFormat "%{User-agent}i" agent
```

Basic Apache configuration (with PHP)

It's Tuesday morning. Your boss Jane rushes into your office and tells you that she needs a new web server set up today for a new client.

The client's domain is www.widgetware.com, a PHP-based groupware application. There's nothing special about this domain setup, aside from the fact that the client needs PHP installed and running alongside it.

You already have a Linux box available for the server, so you install Apache 1.3 and PHP4.

Sample httpd.conf configuration file

The following is a sample httpd.conf configuration file. I've bolded the sections you should pay attention to.

```
# Load basic Apache configuration
Include basic.conf
# Load Modules
Include modules.conf
# Load the PHP module
LoadModule php4_module /usr/lib/apache/1.3/libphp4.so
AddModule mod_php4.c
AddType application/x-httpd-php .php
# Load Logs
Include logfiles.conf
ServerAdmin webmaster@widgetware.com
ServerName www.widgetware.com
DocumentRoot /var/www/
ErrorLog /var/log/apache/error.log
CustomLog /var/log/apache/ access.log combined
<Directory />
Options Indexes SymLinksIfOwnerMatch MultiViews
    AllowOverride None
</Directory>
<Directory /var/www/>
        DirectoryIndex index.php
    Options Indexes Includes FollowSymLinks MultiViews ExecCGI
    AllowOverride All
    Order allow,deny
    Allow from all
</Directory>
```

The first highlighted lines in this code show the PHP module being loaded and added to Apache through the LoadModule and AddModule directives. Following this, you configure Apache to recognize the .php file extension as a PHP file.

The next configuration changes come in the <Directory> section. First, you change the DirectoryIndex directive to point to index.php, instead of index.html. Next, you add the ExecCGI option in order to ensure that the PHP scripts will be executed when run.

9

Slashdotted![1]

You work for Scoot Industries, LLC, which develops ecofriendly transportation. Your company has just released an affordable consumer car powered by vegetable oil, which gets 300 miles to the gallon and doesn't pollute. It has the recommendation of the EPA, Greenpeace, the U.S. Department of Transportation, *and* Michael Moore. It truly is the greatest thing since sliced bread.

And because it's *so* fantastic, it has attracted the attention of news sites everywhere—which of course makes for a lot of traffic coming to your website. As a result, several news organizations have linked to your website, and your poor web server, running under Windows 2000, is working its little heart out.

The problem is that your marketing department has placed several large movie files on the site, in Apple QuickTime format, and they're being requested by just about everybody that's coming to the site. Your dedicated T1 is hitting capacity and connections are being refused when people try to hit the site.

Obviously, you don't want to lose potential customers with a website that's down, but you don't want to be redesigning the site to remove access to the movies either. The secret is to use Apache's mod_rewrite module, to redirect users who are requesting the videos to a page that explains that your website is currently experiencing a heavy amount of traffic, and that the videos aren't available.

Sample httpd.conf configuration file

In the following configuration file, I've bolded the sections that are different from the standard httpd.conf configuration file.

```
# Load basic Apache configuration
Include basic.conf
# Load Modules
Include modules.conf
LoadModule throttle_module /usr/lib/apache/mod_throttle.so
# Load Logs
Include logfiles.conf
ServerAdmin webmaster@scootindustries.com
ServerName www.scootindustries.com
DocumentRoot c:/htdocs
ErrorLog logs/error.log
CustomLog logs/access.log combined
<Directory />
```

[1] Slashdot effect: n. 1. Also known as the "/. effect"; what is said to have happened when a website becomes virtually unreachable because too many people are hitting it after the site was mentioned in an interesting article on the popular Slashdot news service. The term is quite widely used by /. readers, including variants like "That site has been slashdotted again!" —Eric S. Raymond, "The Jargon File, version 4.4.7," home page at www.jargon.org.

```
        Options Indexes SymLinksIfOwnerMatch MultiViews
            AllowOverride None
    </Directory>
    <Directory /htdocs/>
        Options Indexes Includes FollowSymLinks MultiViews
        AllowOverride All
        Order allow,deny
        Allow from all
        <IfModule throttle_module>
            ThrottlePolicy request 10 1s
            ThrottlePolicy speed 100 1s
        </IfModule>
    </Directory>
    # Redirect users from the videos to a "Sorry" page
    <Directory /htdocs/products/scootbot/videos/>
        Options Indexes Includes FollowSymLinks MultiViews ExecCGI
        AllowOverride All
        RewriteEngine on
        RewriteBase /products/scootbot/
        RewriteRule ^videos/.*
    http://www.scootindustries.com/errors/serverbusy.html
    </Directory>
```

First, I've enabled bandwidth throttling through the mod_throttle module, which I discussed in Chapter 5. Second, I enabled the module through the LoadModule directive. Third, in the main <Directory> section, I added a throttling policy that limits the server to ten requests and 100 KB per second. This will help to alleviate some of the pressure on the server's resources. I'll likely keep this in place even after the heavy traffic has dissipated, just in case it happens again.

The rewrite rule is here for a temporary measure, however; I want to remove it once the traffic dies down and things get back to normal. As a result, I've placed the rewrite rules in their own <Directory> section, so I can find it easily later.

The bulk of the rewrite configuration comes in the last three lines of the <Directory> statement. First, you need to turn on the rewriting engine through the RewriteEngine directive. Next, you have to tell Apache what root URL the redirected file or directory lives in, using the RewriteBase directive. I covered the modules responsible for redirecting content in Chapter 3.

The last directive is the rewrite rule itself. For the source in this example, I'm using a wild card to specify that all files within the /products/videos directory on the web server will be redirected to the "server busy" page.

9

Protected intranet directory

Shortly before 3 p.m., Roger saunters over from the human resources office. As he strokes his whiskers, he mentions that they need you to set up an intranet directory on the web server for an employee newsletter. Since the newsletter is going to be talking about successes and failures in the company, it's important that the directory be protected from people outside the network.

OK. Let's assume that addresses in your network follow the 192.168.0.x address format. That is, your IP address on the network might be something like 192.168.0.131, whereas your officemate's IP address might be 192.168.0.132. You'll make use of two Apache features: basic authentication or basic access control.

Since the intranet site is for all employees, the simplest thing to do is use the Order, Allow, and Deny directives to control access to the directory. However, this excludes off-site employees who are checking the site through the Internet. As a result, the best method to use here is a combination of both access control and basic authentication, along with the Satisfy directive.

The Satisfy directive, when set to "any", sets an either/or scenario in Apache; if the user requesting the page is outside the 192.168.0.x IP address range, he'll be presented with a login prompt. Otherwise, the page will be shown to him without having to authenticate on the Apache server.

Sample httpd.conf file

In the following configuration file, I've bolded the sections that are different from the standard httpd.conf configuration file.

```
# Load basic Apache configuration
Include basic.conf
# Load Modules
Include modules.conf
# Load Logs
Include logfiles.conf
ServerAdmin webmaster@staticred.com
ServerName staticred.com
DocumentRoot /var/www/
 ErrorLog /var/log/apache/error.log
CustomLog /var/log/apache/access.log combined
<Directory />
Options Indexes SymLinksIfOwnerMatch MultiViews
    AllowOverride None
</Directory>
<Directory /var/www/>
    Options Indexes Includes FollowSymLinks MultiViews
    AllowOverride All
    Order allow,deny
    Allow from all
```

```
  </Directory>
  <Directory /var/www/intranet/>
    Options Indexes Includes FollowSymLinks MultiViews ExecCGI
    AllowOverride All
    AuthName "Foo Industries Extranet - Employee Access Only"
    AuthType Basic
    AuthUserFile /var/www/intranet/.htpasswd
    Require valid-user
    Order Allow, Deny
    Allow from 192.168.0
    Deny from all
    Satisfy any
    ErrorDocument 401 /errors/authorization.html
  </Directory>
```

In order to maintain this section easily in the future, I've added a special <Directory> section for the protected directory. This will help you find it quicker in the future, should you need to make configuration changes. Because this system is going to be accessed by people outside the company network (hence the name extranet), you won't always know what IP address they're coming from. As a result, you'll want to ask for a username and a password before allowing them access to the site.

The first directive you want to use for configuring authentication is AuthName. This directive will display text in the user's alert box, describing why Apache is requesting that they authenticate before seeing the page. Next, you need to tell Apache what type of authentication to use. As I discussed in Chapter 3, not all browsers support all types of authentication; as a result, you'll want to stick with basic authentication.

After you've told Apache what type of authentication to use, you need to tell it where to find the users allowed on the system. This is the .htpasswd file, which is created through using the htpasswd utility. To bring the authentication together, you finally need to tell Apache that it needs a valid user in order to authenticate.

Because this system is also going to be used inside the network, you don't want to have to force users to log in every time they want to have access to the intranet. As a result, you need to set up an additional access rule based on the IP address of the person visiting.

This is done through the Allow and Deny directives. First, you need to tell Apache the order in which it should read the access rules. In this case, you want it to read the access rules first, followed by the deny rules. This is done through Order, Allow, and Deny. Next, you want to tell Apache which IP addresses it should allow to access the directory. Since everyone in the internal network has an IP address starting with 192.168.0 (for example, 192.168.1.42), you'll set this up with a wild card: Allow from 192.168.0. Next, you have to tell Apache to deny all other IP addresses through the Deny from all directive.

Finally, you have to tell Apache that if either the IP address matches or the user enters the right username and password, the user is allowed access to the directory. This is done through the Satisfy any directive.

9

Running virtual hosts

Jane is back again. It turns out that the client is running three domains, two of which share the same content. The first two domains are www.widgetware.com and www.widgetware.net, which is a site for their WidgetWare product. They also run www.widgetmasters.org, a community support site for their product. Their resources are limited, so they want to share a single server among all of the sites.

For this setup, you'll need to create <VirtualHost> sections for each of the domains and make use of the ServerAlias directive.

Sample httpd.conf configuration file

```
# Load basic Apache configuration
Include basic.conf
# Load Modules
Include modules.conf
# Load Logs
Include logfiles.conf
ServerAdmin webmaster@widgetware.com
ServerName widgetware.com
ServerAlias widgetware.net
DocumentRoot /var/www/widgetware/
ErrorLog /var/log/apache/widgetware-error.log
CustomLog /var/log/apache/widgetware-access.log combined
<Directory />
Options Indexes SymLinksIfOwnerMatch MultiViews
    AllowOverride None
</Directory>
<Directory /var/www/>
    Options Indexes Includes FollowSymLinks MultiViews
    AllowOverride All
    Order allow,deny
    Allow from all
</Directory>
NameVirtualHost 204.174.19.10:80
# widgetmasters.org's configuration
<VirtualHost 204.174.19.10>
  ServerName widgetmasters.org
  ServerAdmin webmaster@widgetmasters.org
  DocumentRoot /var/www/widgetmasters
  ErrorLog /var/log/apache/widgetmasters-error.log
  CustomLog /var/log/apache/widgetmasters-access.log
  <Directory /var/www/widgetmasters>
        Options Indexes Includes FollowSymLinks MultiViews
        AllowOverride All
  </Directory>
  ScriptAlias /cgi-bin/ /var/www/widgetmasters/cgi-bin/
```

```
    <Directory /var/www/widgetmasters/cgi-bin/>
      Options Indexes, Includes, FollowSymLinks, Multiviews, ExecCGI
      AllowOverride All
    </Directory>
  </VirtualHost>
```

As I discussed in Chapter 4, virtual hosts are configured separately from the main domain by using the <VirtualHost> section. In some cases, however, you may need to preface these sections with the NameVirtualHost directive. Other than the <VirtualHost> section heading, however, configuring a virtual host is identical to configuring the main domain name. You still create <Directory> sections within it to specify the options for the main directory, and you configure log files for the virtual hosts.

For more information about virtual hosts, check out Chapter 4.

Compressed HTTP sessions

One of Apache's great features is HTTP compression. This feature, as you may have guessed, compresses the HTML, graphics, and other web files before sending them over the Internet to the browser, which then decompresses the files before displaying them. Many servers have this enabled to save on bandwidth costs. Although you may only save 2 or 3 KB per transfer, it all adds up rather quickly!

Sample httpd.conf configuration file

```
# Load basic Apache configuration
Include basic.conf
# Load Modules
Include modules.conf
# Load Logs
Include logfiles.conf
ServerAdmin webmaster@widgetware.com
ServerName www.widgetware.com
ServerAlias www.widgetware.net
DocumentRoot /var/www/widgetware/
<Directory />
Options Indexes SymLinksIfOwnerMatch MultiViews
    AllowOverride None
</Directory>
<Directory /var/www/>
    Options Indexes Includes FollowSymLinks MultiViews
    AllowOverride All
    Order allow,deny
    Allow from all
</Directory>
<IfModule mod_dir.c>
    DirectoryIndex index.html index.php index.htm index.shtml index.cgi
```

9

```
        </IfModule>
        <IfModule mod_mime.c>
            AddEncoding x-compress Z
            AddEncoding x-gzip gz tgz
            AddIconByEncoding (CMP,/icons/compressed.gif) x-compress x-gzip
            AddType application/x-httpd-php .php
            AddType application/x-httpd-php-source .phps
            AddType application/x-tar .tgz
            <IfModule mod_gzip.c>
              mod_gzip_on                    Yes
              mod_gzip_temp_dir              /tmp/
              mod_gzip_on                    Yes
              mod_gzip_dechunk               Yes
              mod_gzip_minimum_file_size     300
              mod_gzip_maximum_file_size     0
              mod_gzip_maximum_inmem_size    100000
              mod_gzip_keep_workfiles        No
              mod_gzip_add_header_count      No
              mod_gzip_item_include   file     \.htm$
              mod_gzip_item_include   file     \.html$
              mod_gzip_item_include   mime     text/.*
              mod_gzip_item_include   file     \.html$
              mod_gzip_item_include   file     \.jsp$
              mod_gzip_item_include   file     \.php$
              mod_gzip_item_include   file     \.pl$
              mod_gzip_item_include   mime     ^text/.*
              mod_gzip_item_include   mime     ^application/x-httpd-php
              mod_gzip_item_include   mime     ^httpd/unix-directory$
              mod_gzip_item_include   handler  ^perl-script$
              mod_gzip_item_include   handler  ^server-status$
              mod_gzip_item_include   handler  ^server-info$
              mod_gzip_item_exclude   file     \.css$
              mod_gzip_item_exclude   file     \.js$
              mod_gzip_item_exclude   mime     ^image/.*
            </IfModule>
            AddType image/bmp .bmp
            AddHandler cgi-script .cgi .sh .pl
        AddType text/html .shtml
        AddHandler server-parsed .shtml
        </IfModule>
```

It looks like there's a lot going on in this sample, but there really isn't. First, you want to make sure that the mod_mime module is enabled; if it isn't, you can't add the compressed file types. Next, you need to set up the items that should and shouldn't be compressed on the server. Items that should be compressed are included through the mod_gzip_item_include directive, while items that shouldn't be compressed are added through the mod_gzip_item_exclude directive. In the previous case, you want all HTML and text-based files to be compressed, and all image, CSS, and JavaScript files to not be compressed.

Summing it up

The previous samples should give you a heck of a good head start toward configuring your Apache server. Feel free to mix and match the previous configurations to suit your own purposes. Experimenting with your Apache configuration is one of the best ways to learn (just make sure you have backups of the httpd.conf configuration file!).

9

APPENDIX
RESOURCES

This appendix contains many resources that will help you on your way toward becoming an Apache superstar. Refer to the friends of ED website (www.friendsofed.com/) for updates to this list.

Apache documentation

There's a lot of documentation out there for Apache—so much, in fact, that it's hard to decide where to begin. The following are links to some of the most useful Apache resources on the Web.

Official Apache documentation

Documentation for the Apache web server can be found on the Apache website, and is broken into two versions:

- Apache 1.3 documentation: http://httpd.apache.org/docs/
- Apache 2.0 Documentation: http://httpd.apache.org/docs-2.0/

For more information you can go to http://httpd.apache.org/docs-project/.

Apache's frequently asked questions

Apache's FAQ file (http://httpd.apache.org/docs/misc/FAQ.html) holds answers to many, many potential problems that you might experience when configuring Apache.

Apache's tutorials

Apache also hosts a series of tutorials on their site (http://httpd.apache.org/docs/misc/tutorials.html), covering all the major areas of configuration.

Documentation for Mac OS X

Apple has provided some basic documentation on using Apache with Mac OS X (go to http://developer.apple.com/internet/macosx/intro.html). It outlines basic information on Apache configuration and security issues.

Administering your server

If life were easy, you'd only have to worry about maintaining your Apache configuration. Unfortunately, you also have to learn to configure your operating system as well. The following sites will help you:

Linux Network Administrator's Guide

The Linux Network Administrator's Guide (NAG) is a community-supported handbook. The NAG covers several different aspects of Linux networking, such as network and DNS configuration. The NAG can be found online at www.faqs.org/docs/linux_network/.

Mac OS X Server documentation

Apple maintains some great user documentation on their website. The documentation covers several aspects of Mac OS X configuration, including mail, web, and network services. Apple's Mac OS X Server documentation can be found online at www.apple.com/server/documentation/.

Windows 2000 documentation

Microsoft has supplied online documentation for its Windows 2000 operating system. This documentation can be viewed at www.microsoft.com/windows2000/techinfo/proddoc/default.asp.

Windows XP documentation

Microsoft has supplied online documentation for its Windows XP Professional operating system. This documentation can be viewed at www.microsoft.com/windowsxp/using/default.asp.

Programming languages and databases

The next logical step to running your own web server is to start programming scripts on it. Here are some links to get you started.

PHP

PHP is an extremely useful and easy-to-learn web-programming language. Visit www.php.net for more information.

Perl

Perl is the most commonly used web-programming language, and you can find it on virtually any UNIX-based operating system. Visit www.cpan.org for more information.

> *Windows users can find a Perl installation at* www.activestate.com.

SSI

SSI is a simple scripting language that's used to include files and set variables within HTML documents. Apache's SSI tutorial can be found at: http://httpd.apache.org/docs/howto/ssi.html.

MySQL

MySQL is an open-source database based on the SQL database engine. It's an extremely popular choice of database, because of its licensing terms and performance. Go to www.mysql.com for more information.

PostgreSQL

PostgreSQL (www.postgresql.org) is an alternative choice for open-source SQL database engines. Although it isn't as popular or easy to configure, or as user friendly as MySQL, it's every bit as powerful (if not a little more powerful).

OpenSSL

OpenSSL (www.openssl.org) is a free implementation of the SSL protocol and is used in Secure Web. An implementation of OpenSSL for Windows can be found at www.slproweb.com/products/Win32OpenSSL.html.

In order to use OpenSSL in Apache, you need the mod_ssl module, which can be found at www.modssl.org.

Logging

Apache's logging is quite robust—the following links will help you get the best out of your Apache logs.

Configuring logs

For more information on Apache LogLevels, go to http://httpd.apache.org/docs/mod/core.html#loglevel.

For more information on LogRotate, go to www.die.net/doc/linux/man/man8/logrotate.8.html.

Log analysis tools

Analog   www.analog.cx

Webalizer   www.mrunix.net/webalizer/

WebTrends   www.webtrends.com

Virtual hosts

Apache's virtual host documentation can be found online at http://httpd.apache.org/docs/vhosts/.

Kasia's Geek Notes has an excellent virtual host sample configuration. It can be found online at www.unix-girl.com/geeknotes/apache_virtual_host_conf.html.

General tools

Here are several tools you can use once you're more comfortable with Apache and its inner workings.

cPanel

cPanel & WebHost Manager (WHM) (www.cpanel.net) is a commercial-hosting control-panel system, which allows you to graphically configure your Linux server. It's extremely user friendly, but does cost a little money to purchase.

This utility helps make Apache easier to configure and maintain. Instead of opening a shell on the Apache server, editing the configuration files manually, and restarting Apache, you can make changes in an easy-to-use graphical setting.

The problem with this, of course, is that it's web based. This opens you up to a potential breach of security should someone get ahold of your cPanel password, or exploit it in some unforeseen way. It's also possible to misconfigure Apache using the web interface, possibly even blocking your access to fix the problem!

Webmin

Webmin (www.webmin.com) is a web-based interface for system administration for UNIX. Using any browser that supports tables and forms (and Java for the File Manager module), you can set up user accounts, Apache, DNS, file sharing, and so on.

Webmin consists of a simple web server, and a number of CGI programs that directly update system files. For example, look for /etc/inetd.conf and /etc/passwd. The web server and all CGI programs are written in Perl version 5, and use no nonstandard Perl modules.

Webmin offers the same features as cPanel, but is free software. The drawback to Webmin is that it's a little rougher around the edges, and not quite as easy to use. Still, it offers a graphical means of configuring your Linux system. It also supports Mac OS X; as of the writing of this book, cPanel doesn't.

flood

flood (http://httpd.apache.org/test/flood/) is a profile-driven HTTP load tester. In layman's terms, it means that flood is capable of generating large amounts of web traffic. flood's flexibility and power arises in its configuration syntax. It's able to work well with dynamic content.

flood is an excellent tool for testing your web server's performance under heavy usage. It's also useful for testing your mod_throttle policies.

Additional resources

Now that you have some base knowledge of Apache, you can go on and learn more. The following resources will be very helpful.

Apache-tools.com

Apache Tools (www.apache-tools.com/tooltree.jsp) is a compendium of many current tools and information sources for users of the Apache web server.

Apache week

Apache week (www.apacheweek.com) is one of the longest running Apache-specific publications on the Web, and has a wealth of information for both new and advanced Apache users.

Linux user groups

This is a mostly complete list of Linux user groups around the world (go to www.linux.org/groups/). Linux user groups are excellent places to get one-on-one advice and help with both Linux and Apache.

comp.infosystems.www.servers

This newsgroup caters to all web-server software, but it's still a good place to ask questions and get advice.

AFTERWORD
YOU ARE AN APACHE GURU

Welcome to the end of the book.

You've gone through quite the journey! You started off by breaking gently into the world of Apache configuration, through editing the httpd.conf file, then you looked at the inner workings of Apache, and even worked through some pretty complicated stuff, such as configuring SSL and virtual hosts. You can now install, configure, and maintain an Apache server for your organization without fear, and you can go on to do great things.

Keep learning

But your journey isn't over yet. Like with all skills, you must keep learning. Apache is as complicated and full-featured as Photoshop or Illustrator, and while you have a good base of knowledge to work from, there's still a lot to learn.

The Apache documentation is a great place to start. Now that you have enough basic knowledge to find your way around, you'll better understand the more arcane configuration directives and be able to tune your Apache server to your needs.

There are several other resources available to you online, through the Apache website and community websites such as www.apacheweek.com/. Also, don't hesitate to visit Apache newsgroups, or seek out an Apache user group in your area.[1]

Maybe you should even talk to your local propellerhead from time to time. You're now a web god—nothing can stop you!

INDEX